Easy Lotus® No
Release 4.0

Elaine Marmel

Easy Lotus Notes Release 4.0

Copyright © 1996 by Que® Corporation.

International Standard Book Number: 0-7897-0756-X

Library of Congress Catalog Card Number: 95-73259

99 98 97 96   8 7 6 5 4 3 2 1

Interpretation of the printing code: the rightmost number of the first series of numbers is the year of the book's printing; the rightmost number of the second series of numbers is the number of the book's printing. For example, a printing code of 96-1 shows that the first printing of the book occurred in 1996.

Screen reproductions in this book were created by means of the program Collage Complete from Inner Media, Inc., Hollis, NH.

This book was produced digitally by Macmillan Computer Publishing and manufactured by Shepard Poorman Communications Corporation, Indianapolis, Indiana.

Credits

Publisher
Roland Elgey

Vice-President and Publisher
Marie Butler-Knight

Editorial Services Director
Elizabeth Keaffaber

Publishing Manager
Lynn Zingraf

Managing Editor
Michael Cunningham

Acquisitions Coordinator
Martha O'Sullivan

Product Development Specialist
Melanie Palaisa

Production Editor
Mark Enochs

Copy Editor
San Dee Phillips

Technical Editor
Garrett Pease

Book Designer
Barbara Kordesh

Cover Designers
Dan Armstrong
Kim Scott

Technical Specialist
Nadeem Muhammed

Production Team
Claudia Bell
Jason Carr
Anne Dickerson
Brad Dixon
Chad Dressler
Jenny Earhart
Jason Hand
Damon Jordan
Daryl Kessler
Clint Lahnen
Glenn Larsen
Bob LaRoche
Michelle Lee
Bobbi Satterfield
Michael Thomas
Todd Wente
Jody York

Indexer
Craig Small

Composed in *Stone Serif* and *MCPdigital* by Que Corporation

About the Author

Elaine Marmel is President of Marmel Enterprises, Inc., an organization that specializes in technical writing and software training. Elaine spends most of her time writing and is the author of several books on Word for Windows, Word for the Mac, Quicken for Windows, Quicken for DOS, 1-2-3 for Windows, and Excel. Elaine also is a contributing editor to *Inside Timeslips* and *Inside Peachtree for Windows*, monthly magazines published about Timeslips, a time and billing package, and Peachtree for Windows, an accounting package.

Elaine left her native Chicago for the warmer climes of Florida (by way of Cincinnati, OH; Jerusalem, Israel; Ithaca, NY; and Washington, D.C.) where she basks in the sun with her PC and her cats, Cato and Watson. Elaine also sings in the Toast of Tampa, an International Champion Sweet Adeline barbershop chorus.

Acknowledgments

I'd like to thank Martha O'Sullivan for giving me the opportunity to write this book. She was pregnant during the writing of this book and gave birth, at the very end of the project, to a bouncing baby girl. I feel like we went through labor together.

I'd also like to thank Melanie Palaisa for her excellent guidance through this project. You get the "You Kept Me Sane" award, Melanie. As always, it is a pleasure to work with you. Finally, thanks to Mark Enochs who made the author review process run smoothly.

Trademark Acknowledgments

All terms mentioned in this book that are known to be trademarks or service marks have been appropriately capitalized. Que Corporation cannot attest to the accuracy of this information. Use of a term in this book should not be regarded as affecting the validity of any trademark or service mark.

Contents

Part III: Using Notes Databases and Documents   74

Part IV: Creating Your Own Notes Databases 100

Introduction

What You Can Do with Lotus Notes

Lotus Notes is a very flexible product. You can use Notes to communicate with others via electronic mail (*e-mail*). Notes contains built-in multimedia capabilities and provides a document-management system. You can also use Notes to automate work-flow projects and for tracking and discussion purposes. Specifically, Lotus Notes has the following benefits:

- *Multi-platform.* Lotus Notes can run on Macintoshes, Windows, UNIX, and OS/2 machines at the same time and access the same information. Notes depends on *server* machines to hold and organize data, keep track of security and access privileges, share information among all the users, and route documents, files, and information.

- *Notes Mail.* Notes is also a complete electronic mail package. You can easily send messages to and receive messages from any other Notes user on your network. You can attach documents to Notes mail messages and also send files and multimedia messages with audio and video characteristics. Notes Mail is probably the most popular of all Lotus Notes features.

- *Databases.* You can make use of databases that Notes automatically creates for you, such as the Mail database, which holds all your mail messages. And, because Notes databases are "free-form" containers of information, you might use a Notes database that contains documents that discuss a particular topic. This type of database is a *discussion group* database. Finally, your company may use Notes to store information such as *forms* that are used company-wide.

- *Text searching and indexing.* You can quickly search large amounts of information for specific items within a database. Notes uses an indexing feature that keeps track of the information added to a database, and you can configure Notes to keep these indexes up to date.

- *Database replication.* Replication allows you to copy one database across multiple Notes servers. If you have a database that lists all of the employees of your company, you might want that database replicated to all your servers in your Notes network. Replication allows all of the servers to have the same version of your database. If you make an update or a change to the database on any server in your Notes network, that change will be replicated throughout your whole network so that everyone can see the change.

You also can replicate all or part of a database from the server to your own computer. That way, you can work in the database when you're not connected to the Notes server. Later, you can replicate your local database back to the server to update the database on the server. This technique is particularly useful for those who work away from the office.

- *Security*. Lotus Notes has a strong, highly integrated security system that limits the number of people who can use your Notes networks, which databases they can access, and even which parts of the database they can read or access.

- *Internet Access*. With Notes Release 4.0, you can access the Internet. Connecting to and using the Internet is a large topic—and beyond the scope of this book. If you want to use the Internet, see your Notes Administrator for instructions.

Basic Notes Concepts

Before you start reading this book, you should become familiar with a few basic terms. Once you understand those terms, you should be ready to start learning how to use Notes!

Notes uses the term *database* to refer to compartmentalized information in a single area of interest that you might want to share. This concept is really important, because Notes databases are not like traditional databases. For purposes of understanding databases in Notes, you can think of databases as containers that hold similar information. When you create a new database, you can customize and personalize your database to use almost any type of information.

A *view* is the fundamental way to see information in a Notes database. Views summarize Notes documents in an easy-to-read format. You can customize views and use them to see different pieces of information in documents. Views are particularly useful for managing your documents, since you can see a list of all available documents to update, add, or delete.

Notes databases store information in *documents*. You create Notes documents that are based on forms that contain specific fields.

A *form* is a customizable screen that is the basis of every document. The appearance of a Notes document depends on the form. Some forms have body and date fields, and others require specific words or user names. Each database has its own forms based on how the database will be used.

Finally, a *field* is the basic unit to store information in Notes. You'll find various types of fields on forms for text, dates, numbers, and graphics.

Task Sections

The Task sections include numbered steps that tell you how to accomplish certain tasks such as sending a mail message or creating a document. The numbered steps walk you through a specific example so you can learn the task by doing it.

Big Screen

At the beginning of each task is a large screen that shows how the computer screen will look after you complete the procedure that follows in that task. Sometimes, the screen shows a feature discussed in that task, however, such as a shortcut menu.

"Why Would I do This?"

Each task includes a brief explanation of why you would benefit from knowing how to accomplish the task.

TASK 4

Using SmartIcons

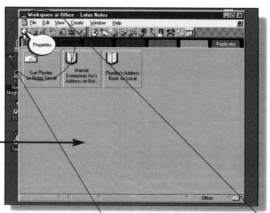

"Why would I do this?"

SmartIcons provide an alternative, shorter way to choose a command in Notes. You must use the mouse to choose a SmartIcon. By default, SmartIcons appear under the Notes menu bar. When you use a SmartIcon, you don't have to pull down a menu and choose a command; you simply click the SmartIcon. To determine the purpose of any particular SmartIcon, use the mouse to point at it; Notes will display a bubble describing the SmartIcon's purpose.

Step-by-Step Screens

Each task includes a screen shot for each step of a procedure. The screen shot shows how the computer screen will look at each step in the process.

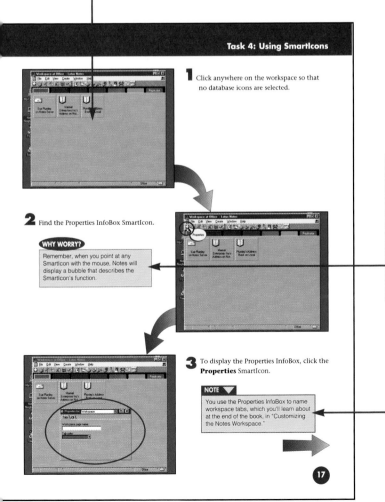

1 Click anywhere on the workspace so that no database icons are selected.

2 Find the Properties InfoBox SmartIcon.

WHY WORRY?

Remember, when you point at any SmartIcon with the mouse, Notes will display a bubble that describes the SmartIcon's function.

3 To display the Properties InfoBox, click the **Properties** SmartIcon.

NOTE

You use the Properties InfoBox to name workspace tabs, which you'll learn about at the end of the book, in "Customizing the Notes Workspace."

17

Why Worry? Notes

You may find that you performed a task that you didn't want to do after all. The Why Worry notes tell you how to undo certain procedures or get out of a situation you didn't mean to get into.

Other Notes

Many tasks contain other short notes that tell you a little more about certain procedures. These notes define terms, explain other options, refer you to other sections when applicable, and so on.

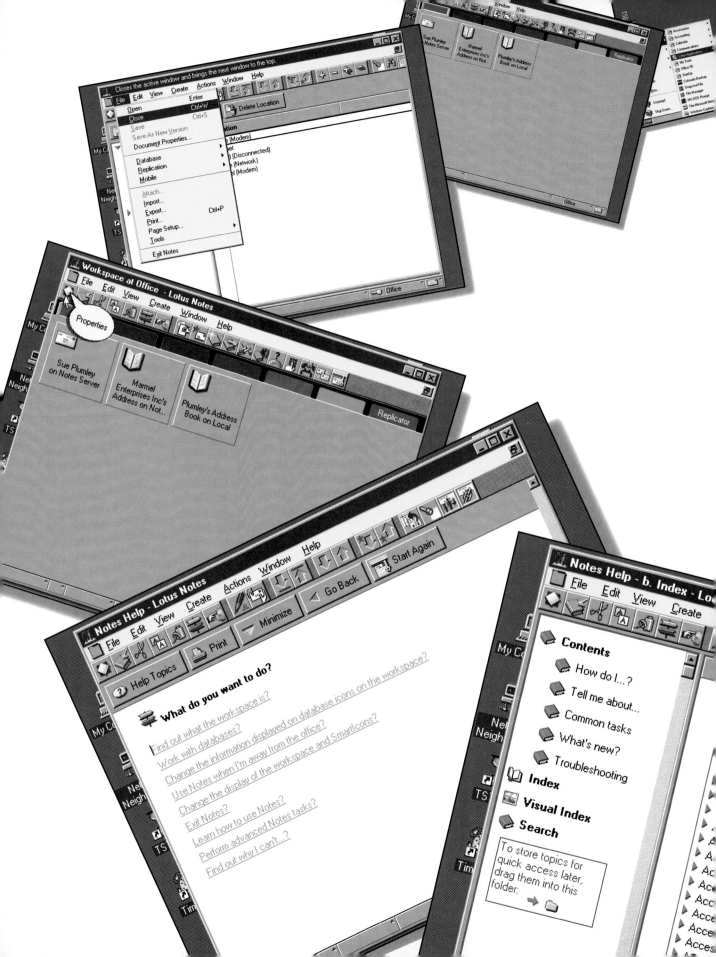

PART I

Lotus Notes Basics

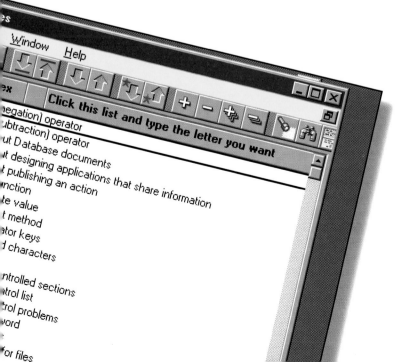

Part I of this book introduces you to Lotus Notes. You learn how to start and exit Notes, how to navigate within Notes, and how to use Notes Help functions. You also learn how to change the size of the Notes window.

To start Lotus Notes, you should have the program installed on your hard disk. We have included a set of installation steps at the back of the book for installing Notes on a workstation running Windows 95 operating system. If you need help installing Lotus Notes on your hard drive, see your systems administrator or the documentation for the program. Once Notes is installed, make sure that Microsoft Windows is running. Notes will probably appear in the Lotus Applications folder when you highlight **Programs** on the Start menu. Once Notes is running, you can take advantage of Windows features, such as using the Clipboard and accessing a central printer.

When you first start Notes, you'll see the Notes workspace. The Notes Workspace consists of a series of tabs called *workspace pages*. You use these workspace pages to organize the databases you use in Notes.

You move around in Notes using either the keyboard or the mouse. Although you can perform most of the tasks with keyboard commands, you will probably prefer the mouse, because the mouse makes it easy to access the various parts of Notes. With the mouse, you can select different ways to view the information in your databases (called database views), access and read documents, and maneuver through the various Notes screens. *SmartIcons* appear toward the top of the Notes screen. SmartIcons are shortcuts that save you time when you perform commands such as opening a database, sending mail, and underlining text. You click a SmartIcon with the mouse to perform the command.

Notes also contains Help. If you would like more information about any screen or prompt within Notes, help is only a single keystroke away—just press **F1**. The Help information answers general questions about the current screen or prompt.

In addition to the single-key Help, Notes includes an indexed Help database. You can search this database for any Notes-related topic or command. The Notes Help index offers thorough descriptions of almost all the features and commands in Notes. Using your mouse, you can scroll through a directory of all available topics to find the desired Notes Help entry.

You also can search the Help database for entries using full or partial text strings. The Notes Help index is a great reference tool for learning how to access many of the intermediate and advanced features of Lotus Notes.

As in most other Windows programs, you can control and resize the Notes window. You can minimize, maximize, and resize as you like.

The tasks that follow teach you the basic skills you need to use Lotus Notes effectively.

Starting Lotus Notes

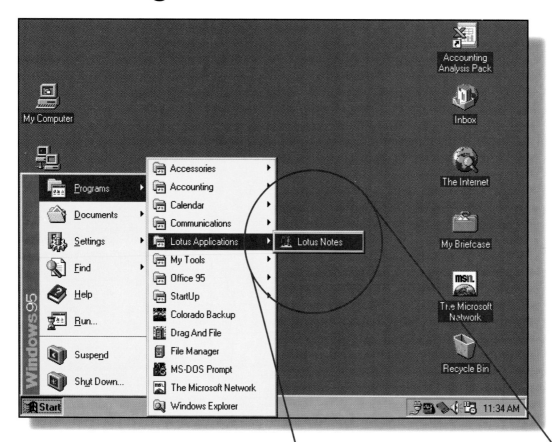

"Why would I do this?"

In Windows 95, you start Lotus Notes from the Programs menu on the Start menu. Typically, the installation process places Notes in the Lotus Applications Folder.

In this task, you'll learn how to start Notes. Start your computer and look at the Windows 95 Desktop.

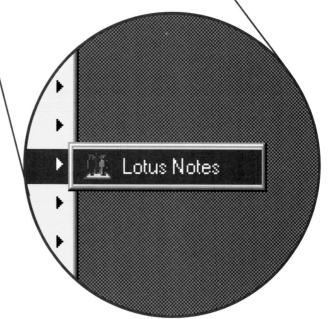

1 Click the **Start** button to display the Start menu.

WHY WORRY?

If you load wallpapers when you load Windows 95, your Desktop background may look different than what you see in the figures in this task.

2 Slide the mouse onto the **Programs** menu. Windows displays the Programs menu choices, which will be different on each computer. The choices on the Programs menu depend on the programs loaded on your computer.

3 Highlight the **Lotus Notes** folder. Typically, you'll find Notes in the Lotus Applications folder. Click **Lotus Notes** once with the left mouse button. Notes starts, and the Notes workspace appears on-screen. You learn more about the workspace in the next task. ∎

Understanding Workspace Pages

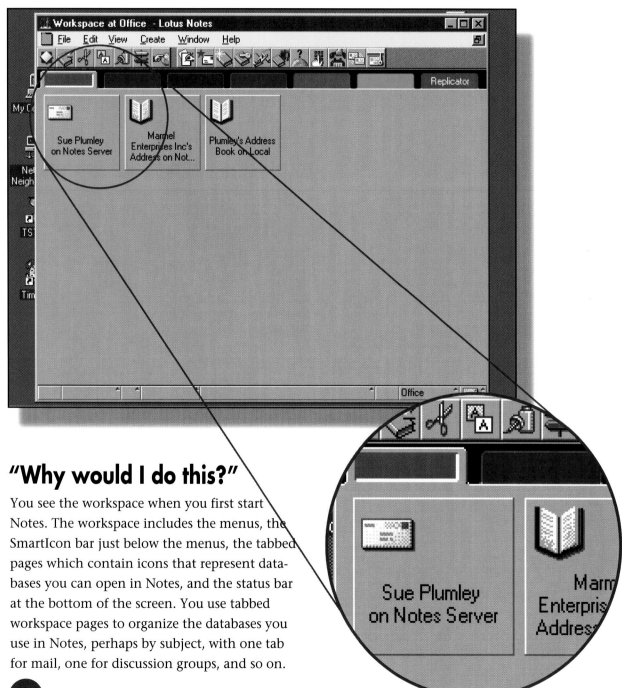

"Why would I do this?"

You see the workspace when you first start Notes. The workspace includes the menus, the SmartIcon bar just below the menus, the tabbed pages which contain icons that represent databases you can open in Notes, and the status bar at the bottom of the screen. You use tabbed workspace pages to organize the databases you use in Notes, perhaps by subject, with one tab for mail, one for discussion groups, and so on.

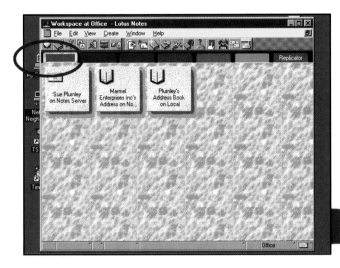

1 The first workspace page contains mail-related database icons: your mail database, the server address book, and your personal address book.

NOTE ▼

Your workspace appears textured like the workspace in this figure. For clarity in the book, we turned off texturing of the workspace. To learn how to turn texturing on and off, see Task 73, "Changing Your Workspace Back ground."

2 Click the tab of a workspace page to display the contents of that page. ■

WHY WORRY?

When you first start using Notes, only the first tab and the Replicator tab will contain icons. Later, you'll learn how to use the other tabs to organize your workspace.

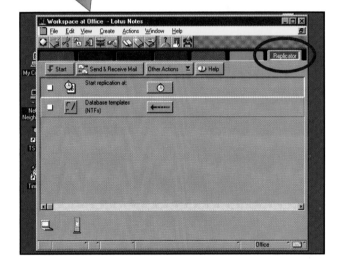

Navigating in Notes

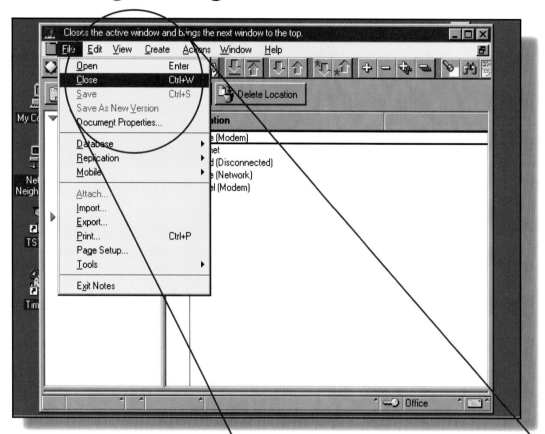

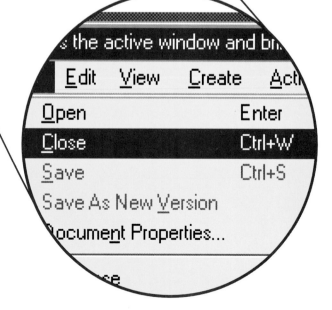

"Why would I do this?"

While you can use either the keyboard or the mouse to navigate through Notes, navigation is faster and easier with the mouse. To use the keyboard, you'll use the underscored letters (called *hot keys*) you see in menu and command names. In this task, you'll learn to open menus, choose commands, and open and close your personal address book, which is a Notes database. Both keyboard and mouse methods are in this task, but in future tasks, you'll use the "easiest" method available.

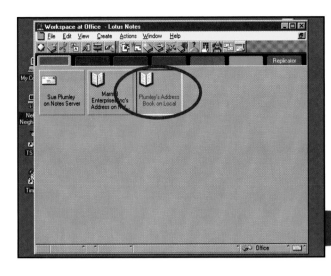

1 Select your personal address book database. Using the mouse, click the icon in the workspace. The title of the address book appears in blue. Your personal address book contains your name and the words **on Local**. In the figure, **Plumley's Address Book on Local** is the personal address book.

WHY WORRY?

If you open the wrong menu, press Esc to close the menu and press a different hot key.

2 Open your personal address book database. With the mouse, double-click the icon for your personal address book database. Using the keyboard, press **Enter** to open the selected database.

WHY WORRY?

Later, you'll learn about other databases. Good news: you open every database the same way.

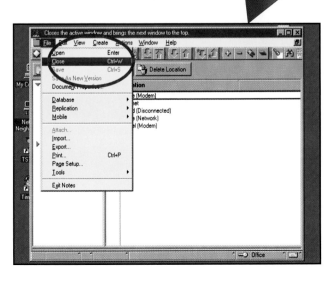

3 To close the database, open the **File** menu by pressing the **Alt** key and then pressing **F**, the hot key in the menu name. Next, choose the **Close** command from the menu by highlighting the command using the up or down arrow key and then pressing **Enter**. ∎

Using SmartIcons

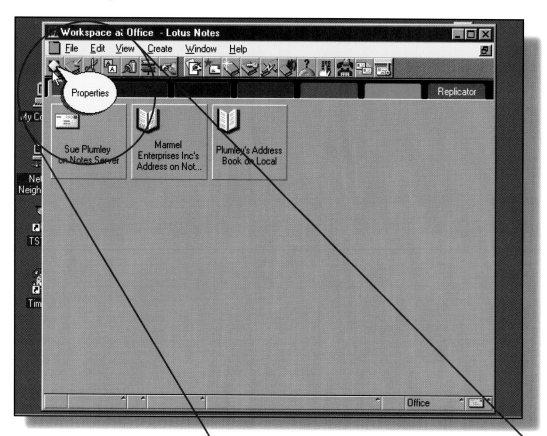

"Why would I do this?"

SmartIcons provide an alternative, shorter way to choose a command in Notes. You must use the mouse to choose a SmartIcon. By default, SmartIcons appear under the Notes menu bar. When you use a SmartIcon, you don't have to pull down a menu and choose a command; you simply click the SmartIcon. To determine the purpose of any particular SmartIcon, use the mouse to point at it; Notes will display a bubble describing the SmartIcon's purpose.

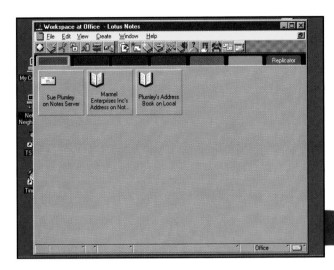

1 Click anywhere on the workspace so that no database icons are selected.

2 Find the Properties InfoBox SmartIcon.

WHY WORRY?

Remember, when you point at any SmartIcon with the mouse, Notes will display a bubble that describes the SmartIcon's function.

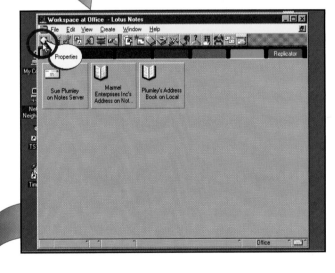

3 To display the Properties InfoBox, click the **Properties** SmartIcon.

NOTE ▼

You use the Properties InfoBox to name workspace tabs, which you'll learn about at the end of the book, in "Customizing the Notes Workspace."

17

4 Close the Properties InfoBox by clicking the **X** in the upper right corner of the Properties InfoBox.

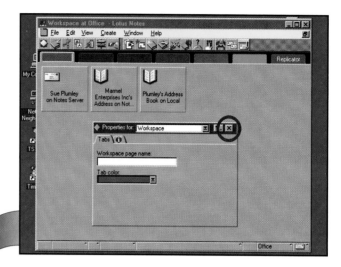

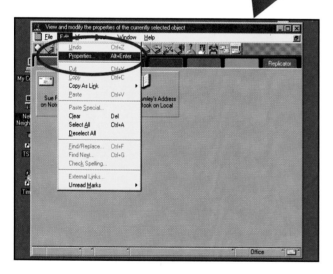

5 To open the Properties InfoBox using the menus, you would click anywhere on the workspace to make sure no database is selected and then open the **Edit** menu and choose the **Properties** command. ■

Using Notes Help

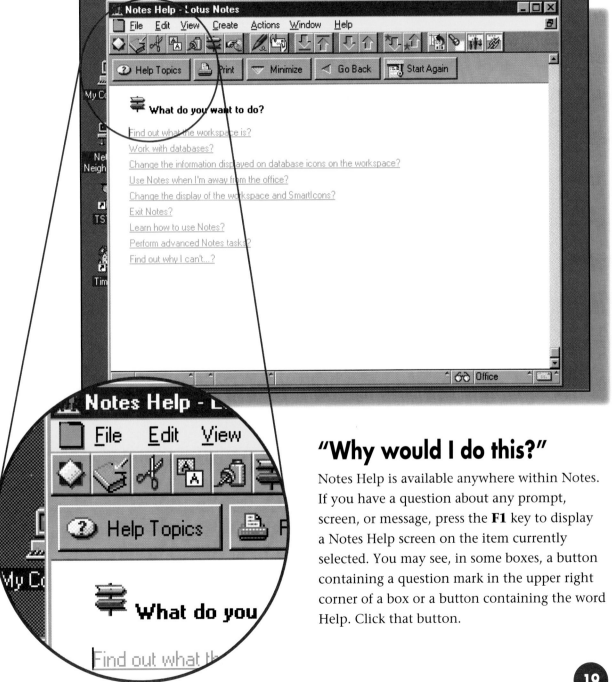

"Why would I do this?"

Notes Help is available anywhere within Notes. If you have a question about any prompt, screen, or message, press the **F1** key to display a Notes Help screen on the item currently selected. You may see, in some boxes, a button containing a question mark in the upper right corner of a box or a button containing the word Help. Click that button.

1 Click anywhere on the gray Notes workspace to select it.

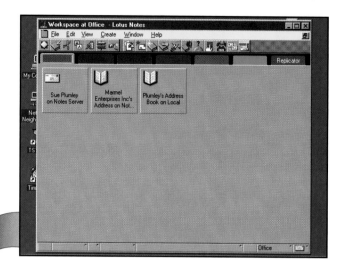

2 Press the **F1** key to request help on the item you have selected: the Notes workspace. Notes Help displays the Help window and a list of help topics, underlined in green, pertaining to the item you selected.

WHY WORRY?

Because the Help database is stored on the server, you may need to type your password to access it. If you already entered your password during the current work session, you may not need to enter it again.

3 To display the help associated with any topic, double-click that topic. ■

NOTE ▼

To close the help screen, press Ctrl+W, or open the File menu and choose the Close command. You'll see the Notes Help database added to the workspace tab.

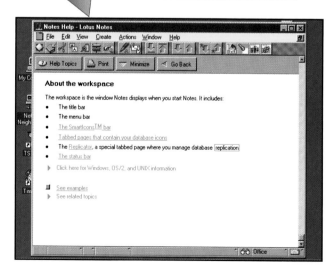

Using the Notes Help Index

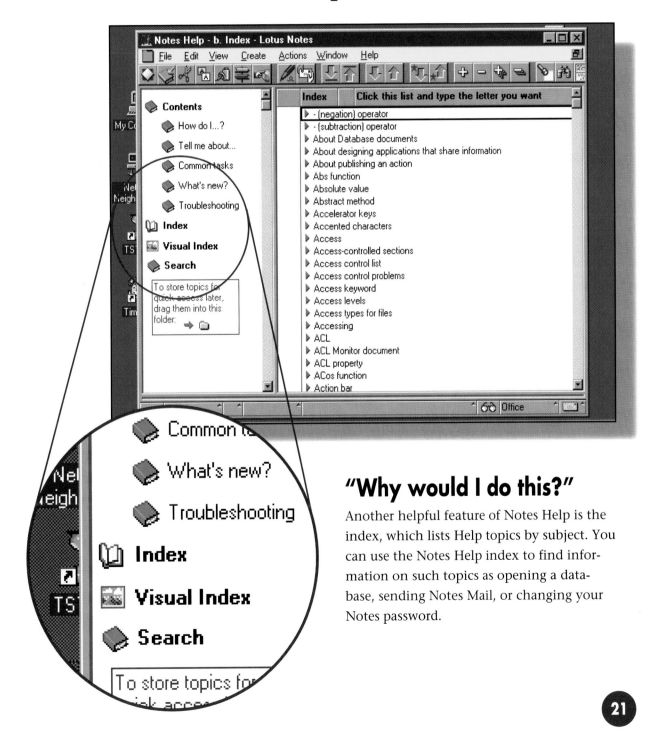

"Why would I do this?"

Another helpful feature of Notes Help is the index, which lists Help topics by subject. You can use the Notes Help index to find information on such topics as opening a database, sending Notes Mail, or changing your Notes password.

1 Double-click the Notes Help database icon or open the **Help** menu and choose **Help Topics**. Notes displays the Help window. Down the left side, you see books with titles next to them. The open book is the Index. Use the scroll bar at the right edge of the screen to move the topics in the window until you see a topic that interests you.

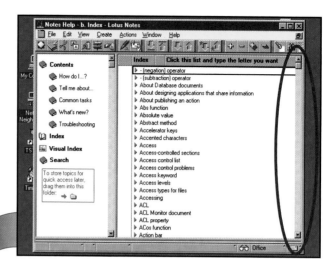

2 Click the arrow next to the topic to see the list of available help topics.

NOTE ▼

You may also see another arrow when you double-click. That indicates additional topics are available; think of these as subtopics.

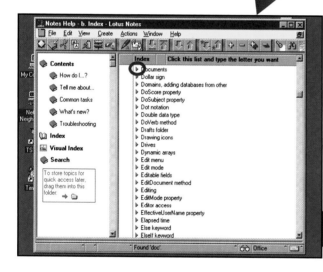

3 To display a help document, double-click the small document icon next to the topic in the right side of the window. The document icon looks like a piece of paper.

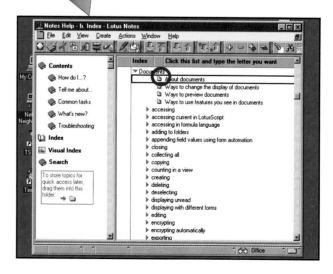

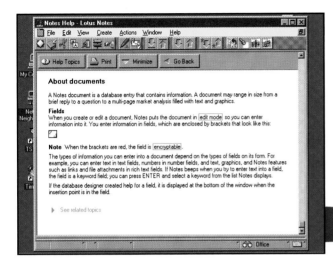

4 Notes displays the Help document you selected in the window.

5 To see the list of topics related to the document you opened, click **See related topics** at the bottom of the document window. ■

NOTE ▼

When you finish reading the document, press Ctrl+W or open the File menu and choose the Close command. To close the Help database, press Ctrl+W again or open the File menu and choose the Close command again.

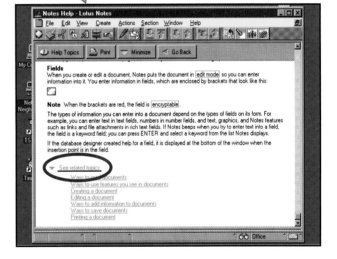

Searching Help

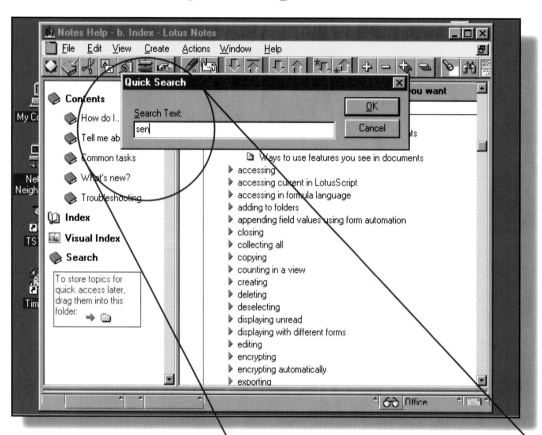

"Why would I do this?"

Sometimes, it's faster to search through Help instead of scrolling and looking at topics. You can perform these more direct types of searches in Notes Help. Let's search for help on mail.

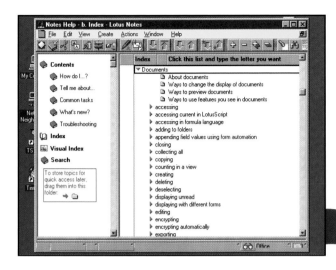

1 Open the **Help** menu and choose **Help Topics**. Notes displays the Help window. Down the left side, you see books with titles next to them. Help displays the last window you viewed in Help.

NOTE ▼

Since Help is a database in Notes, you can open it by double-clicking the Help icon in your workspace.

2 Type the first few letters of the topic for which you want to search. In the example, I typed **sen**. When you type, Notes displays the Quick Search dialog box containing the letters you typed. If you want to narrow the search further, type additional characters.

WHY WORRY?

When you finish, open the File menu and choose the Close command twice to close the Help document and the Help database.

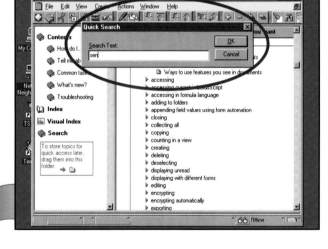

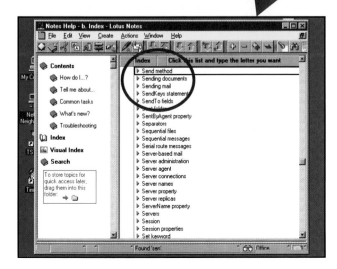

3 When the Quick Search dialog box contains the letters for which you want to search, choose **OK**. In the window on the right, Notes displays the title of the first subject that matches the letters you typed in the Quick Search dialog box. ■

Changing the Size of the Notes Window

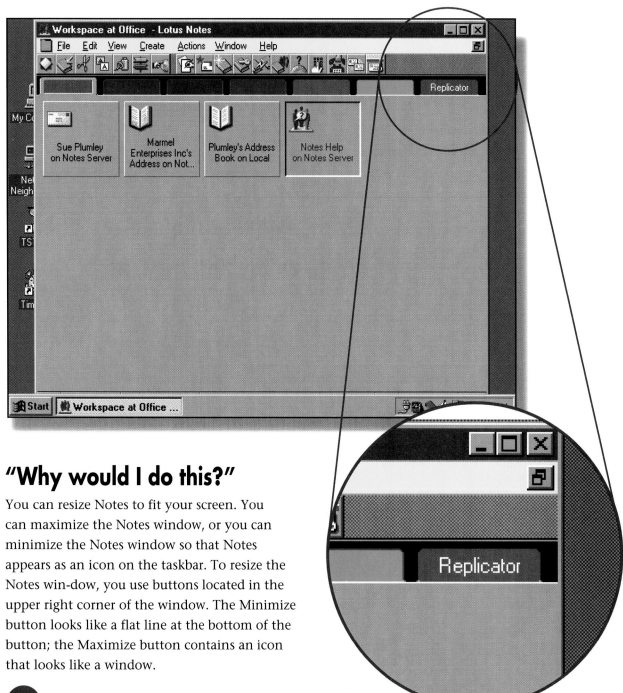

"Why would I do this?"

You can resize Notes to fit your screen. You can maximize the Notes window, or you can minimize the Notes window so that Notes appears as an icon on the taskbar. To resize the Notes win-dow, you use buttons located in the upper right corner of the window. The Minimize button looks like a flat line at the bottom of the button; the Maximize button contains an icon that looks like a window.

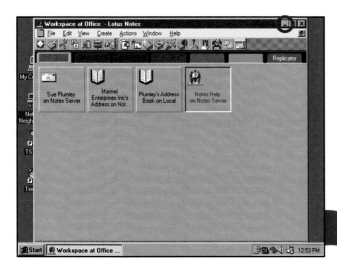

1 Click the **Minimize** button once. Notes appears only as a button titled Workspace at Office on the taskbar at the bottom of the screen.

2 To display the Notes window again, click the **Notes** button in the taskbar at the bottom of the screen. The Notes window appears on-screen again.

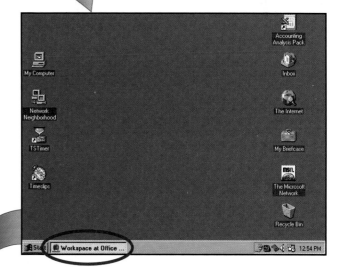

3 To enlarge Notes so that it fills the entire screen, click the **Maximize** button. The icon on the Maximize button is intended to look like a window with a title bar.

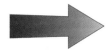

4 When you click the **Maximize** icon, Notes fills the screen, and Windows replaces the Maximize button with the Restore button. ■

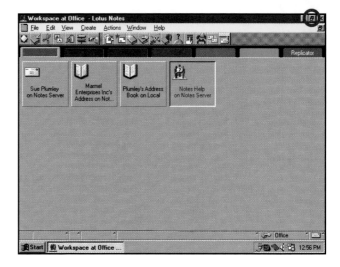

Exiting Lotus Notes

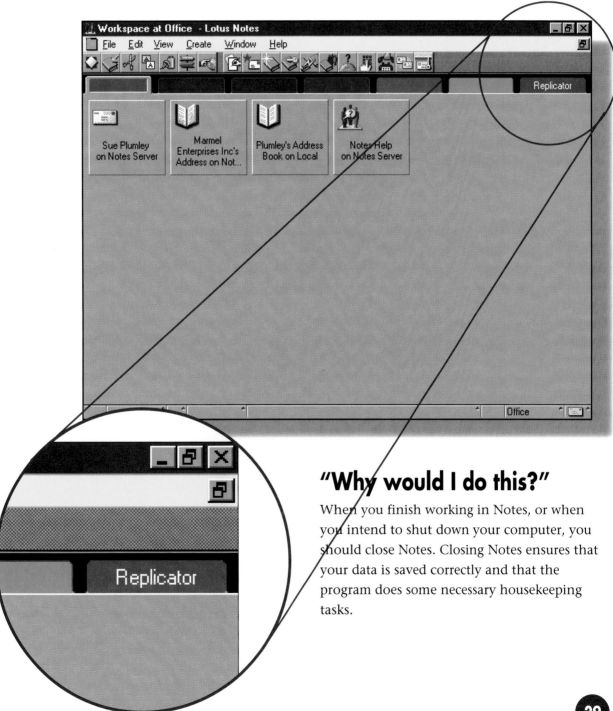

"Why would I do this?"

When you finish working in Notes, or when you intend to shut down your computer, you should close Notes. Closing Notes ensures that your data is saved correctly and that the program does some necessary housekeeping tasks.

1 If you have any databases open, close them by opening the **File** menu and choosing the **Close** command.

WHY WORRY?

If you have open or unsaved documents, Notes will remind you to save the documents before you exit the program.

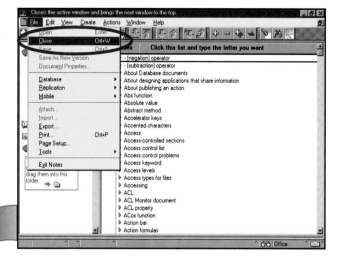

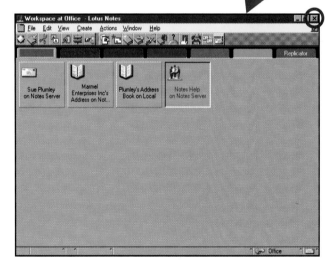

2 To close the program, click the **X** in the upper right corner of the screen. Notes shuts down and Windows redisplays the Desktop. ■

NOTE ▼

You can also close Notes by clicking File in the menu bar and then clicking Exit Notes. This step chooses the File Exit command.

PART II
Using Notes Mail

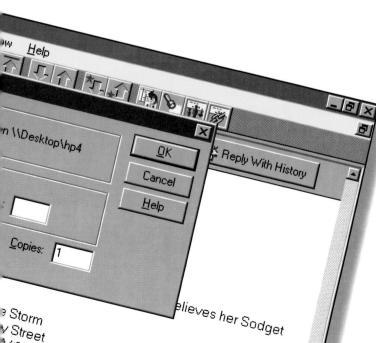

Now that you are familiar with the basics of Lotus Notes, you can start taking advantage of specific Notes features. One of the most important features is e-mail, referred to as Notes Mail.

In Part II, you learn about Notes Mail. You learn how to open your personal mail database, view and read your messages, and organize your messages. You also learn how to use Notes Mail to print mail messages, share documents, respond to messages, forward mail to other Notes users, create a new mail message, and send carbon copies of a message.

Your Notes mail is a unique database in your workspace; only you can access it. It does, however, have some characteristics in common with all Notes databases. For example, most of the time, the screen divides into two panes. The pane on the left, the Navigation pane, shows available views. Notes doesn't use the traditional folder icon for all of these views; for example, the Inbox appears as a tray. The pane on the right, the View pane, shows the contents of a particular view. As you click an icon in the Navigation pane, both the menus at the top of the screen and the view pane will change. And, sometimes, you'll also see a preview pane at the bottom of the screen. The Preview pane lets you look at a document you highlight in the View pane—without opening the document. You'll learn more about views in Part III.

When you start getting a lot of mail, you'll need to know how to organize your mail messages. You can place mail in folders (either folders already available or folders you create) for future reference or delete unnecessary letters. You also can sort incoming and outgoing mail by size, date, sender, and category, making it easier for you to locate a particular mail message later.

Any time you delete a message, Lotus Notes initially marks the message for deletion instead of immediately deleting it, which prevents you from accidentally deleting messages. Whenever you empty the trash or close a database with messages marked for deletion, Notes prompts you for confirmation before deleting the message.

You are not restricted to sending mail messages using Notes Mail; you can use Notes Mail to send any document in any database to any other user of Notes Mail. When you forward a document, a regular mail message appears on-screen with the forwarded document in the body of the memo.

In this part, you'll learn how to add entries to your Address Book database—a useful feature when you regularly exchange mail with particular individuals. You'll also learn how to set up a mailing list for groups to whom you regularly send mail.

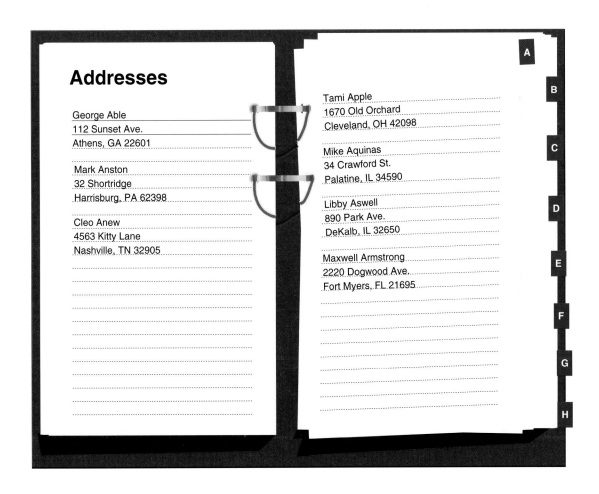

Addresses

George Able
112 Sunset Ave.
Athens, GA 22601

Mark Anston
32 Shortridge
Harrisburg, PA 62398

Cleo Anew
4563 Kitty Lane
Nashville, TN 32905

Tami Apple
1670 Old Orchard
Cleveland, OH 42098

Mike Aquinas
34 Crawford St.
Palatine, IL 34590

Libby Aswell
890 Park Ave.
DeKalb, IL 32650

Maxwell Armstrong
2220 Dogwood Ave.
Fort Myers, FL 21695

A
B
C
D
E
F
G
H

Viewing Your Mail

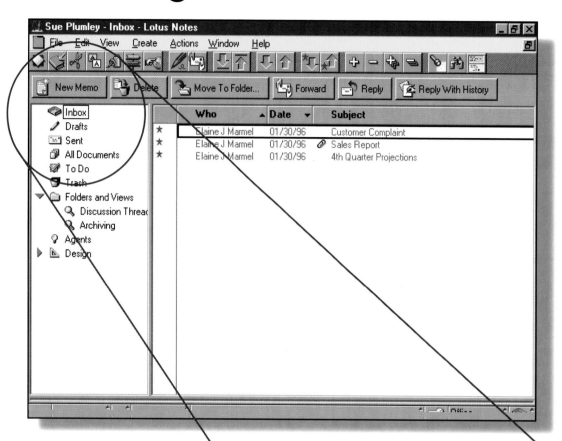

"Why would I do this?"

You must open your mail database to see mail messages you have received. Once you open your mail database, you can read, edit, and sort your personal mail messages because all your mail is sent there. This arrangement keeps all the mail you receive in one central location and makes it easier for you to keep track of your mail.

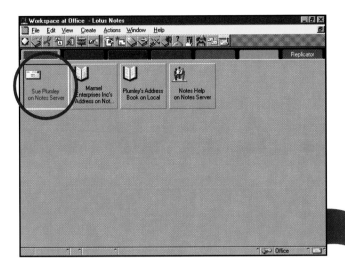

1 Double-click on the icon containing an envelope; it probably also contains your name. That's your mail database icon.

NOTE ▼

Because your mail database is stored on the server, you may need to type in your password to access it. If you already entered your password during the current work session, you may not need to enter it again because Notes will remember your password.

2 The very first time you open your Notes mail database, you'll see a screen similar to this one, describing the purpose of the mail database.

WHY WORRY?

If you need to see the instructions on the screen again, click the database to select it on the workspace tab, open the Help menu, and choose About this Database.

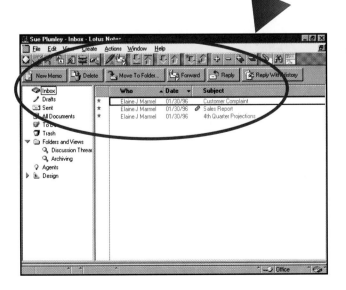

3 Open the **File** menu and choose the **Close** command. Notes then displays the mail database. In the Navigation pane on the left side of the window, you see various views available in the mail database, such as the Inbox. The right side of the screen shows you the contents of a particular view. ■

TASK 11
Opening and Closing Mail

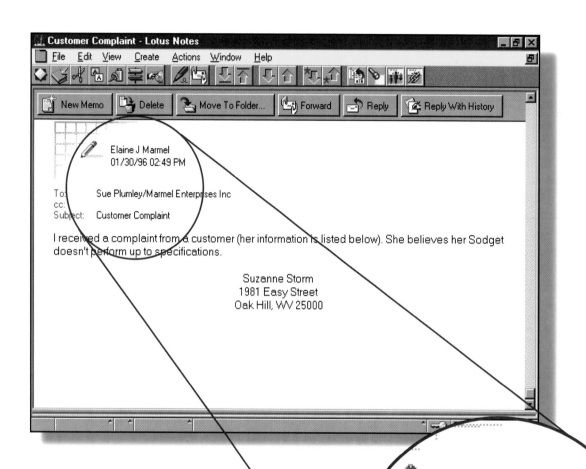

"Why would I do this?"

Without meaning to state the obvious, when you receive mail, you'll probably want to read it; and to read a mail message, you'll need to open it.

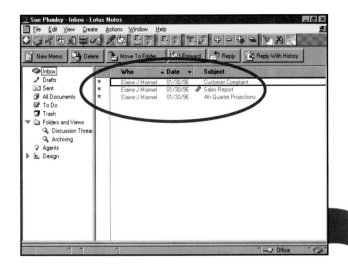

1 Make sure you have your mail database open. Click the **Inbox** in the Navigation pane on the left side of the screen. In the View pane on the right side of the screen, you'll see mail messages waiting for you, who sent them, and the date and subject of each message.

NOTE ▼

A mail message listed in red with a star next to it identifies a message you have never read.

2 Double-click the message you want to read. Notes displays the message on-screen.

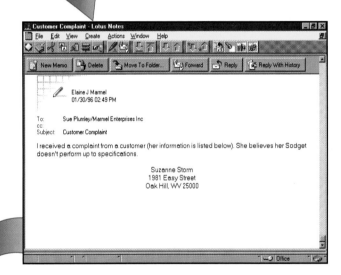

3 When you finish reading the message, close it by opening the **File** menu and choosing the **Close** command. ■

WHY WORRY?

Notice the star has disappeared from the message you opened. Also, the message is no longer listed in red.

TASK 12

Opening a Mail Message Containing an Attached Document

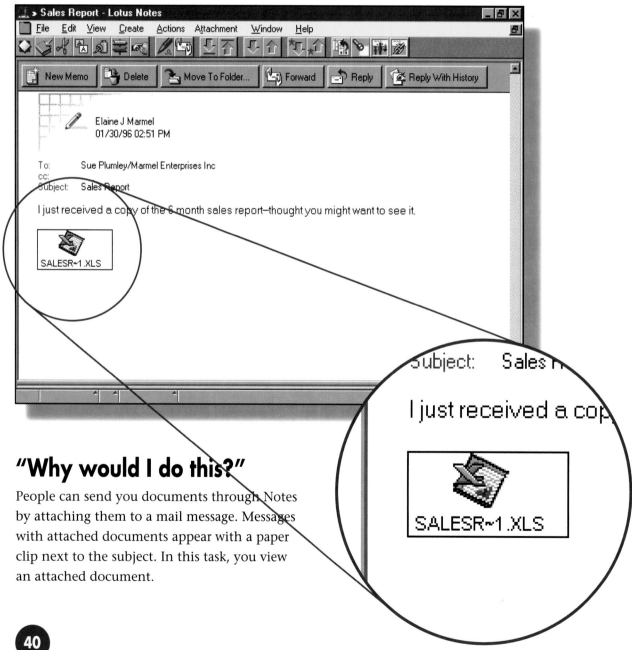

"Why would I do this?"

People can send you documents through Notes by attaching them to a mail message. Messages with attached documents appear with a paper clip next to the subject. In this task, you view an attached document.

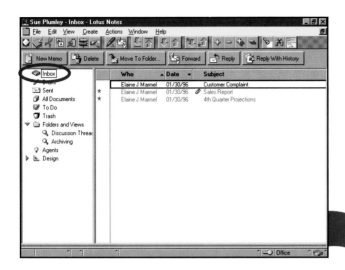

1 Open your mail database and click the **Inbox** to display incoming messages.

2 Double-click a document that contains a paper clip next to the subject.

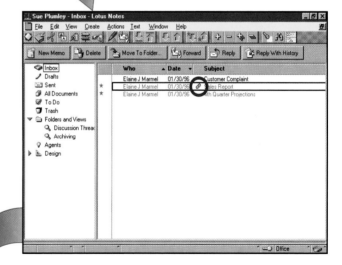

3 Notes displays the document and you see an icon that represents the attached document.

4 Point the mouse at the attachment and press the *right* mouse button to display a shortcut menu. Choose the **View** command.

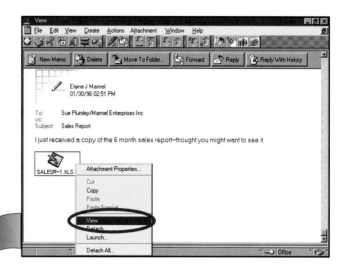

5 Notes launches a viewer that lets you see, but not change, the contents of the attached document.

NOTE ▼

If the viewer doesn't handle the attached document type, it will attempt to launch the application associated with it. You'll learn about launching later in this part.

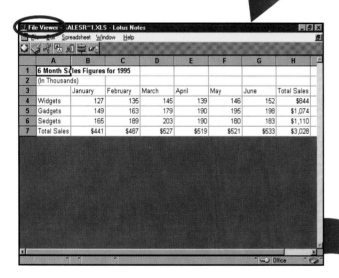

6 To close this window and return to the mail message, open the **File** menu and choose **Close**. ■

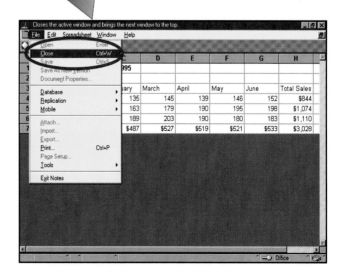

Detaching an Attached Document

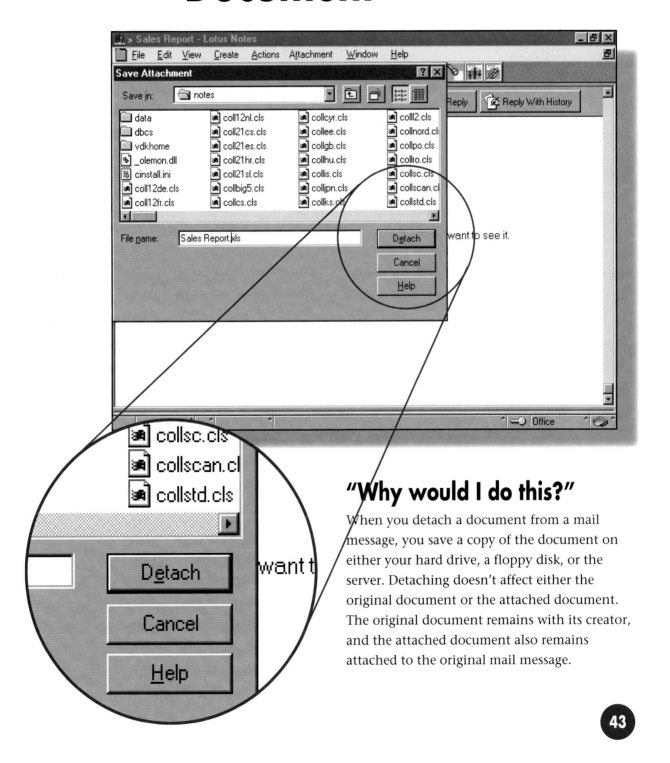

"Why would I do this?"

When you detach a document from a mail message, you save a copy of the document on either your hard drive, a floppy disk, or the server. Detaching doesn't affect either the original document or the attached document. The original document remains with its creator, and the attached document also remains attached to the original mail message.

1 In your mail database, open a mail message that contains a paper clip next to the subject. Point the mouse at the attachment and press the *right* mouse button to display a shortcut menu. Choose the **Detach** command.

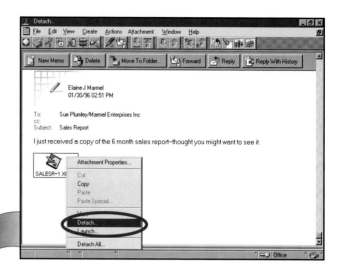

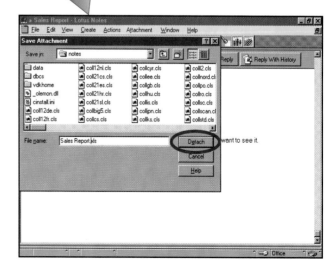

2 Notes displays the Save Attachment dialog box. Use the Save in list box and the File name text box to provide a file name and location where you want to save the detached copy of the file.

3 Choose the **Detach** button. Notes saves a copy of the attachment using the name and location you provided and redisplays the mail message. ■

Launching an
Attached Document

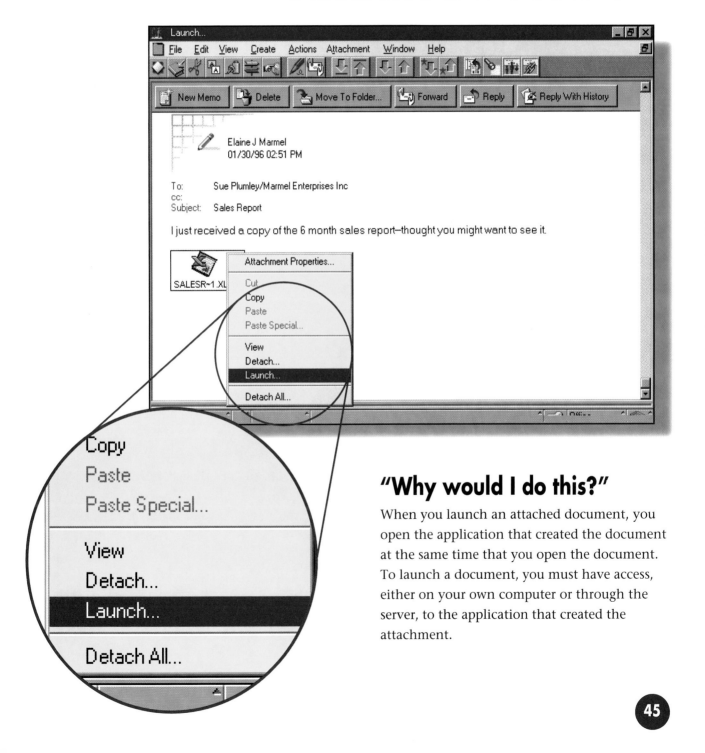

"Why would I do this?"

When you launch an attached document, you open the application that created the document at the same time that you open the document. To launch a document, you must have access, either on your own computer or through the server, to the application that created the attachment.

1 In your mail database, open a mail message that contains a paper clip next to the subject.

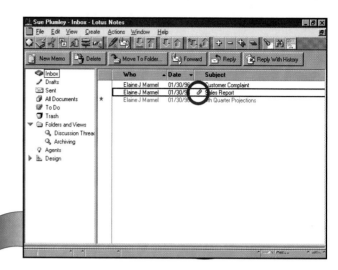

2 Point the mouse at the attachment and press the *right* mouse button to display a shortcut menu. Choose the **Launch** command.

3 The attached document opens in the application that created it. ■

WHY WORRY?

When you finish working with the document, use the application's Exit command to close the application. You'll return to the Notes mail message containing the attached document.

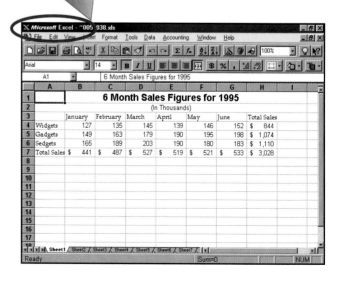

Printing a Mail Message

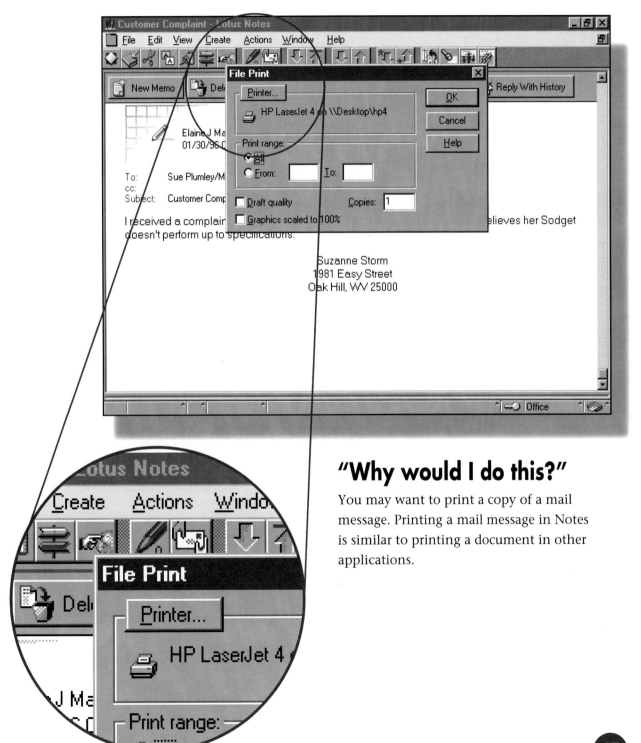

"Why would I do this?"

You may want to print a copy of a mail message. Printing a mail message in Notes is similar to printing a document in other applications.

1 In your mail database, open the message you want to print.

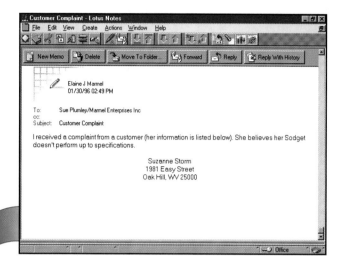

2 Open the **File** menu and choose the **Print** command.

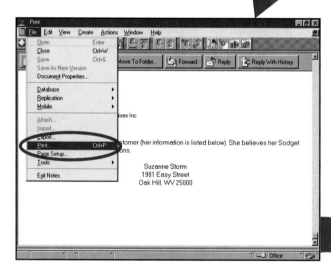

WHY WORRY?

If your printer supports graphics, you'll see virtually the same image on paper that you see on-screen.

3 Notes displays the File Print dialog box. When you choose **OK**, the mail message prints. ■

NOTE ▼

If you print a document that contains an attachment, you'll see a placeholder for the attachment in the printed message.

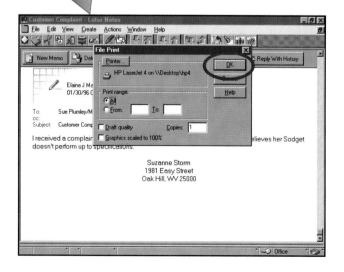

Organizing Your Mail Messages

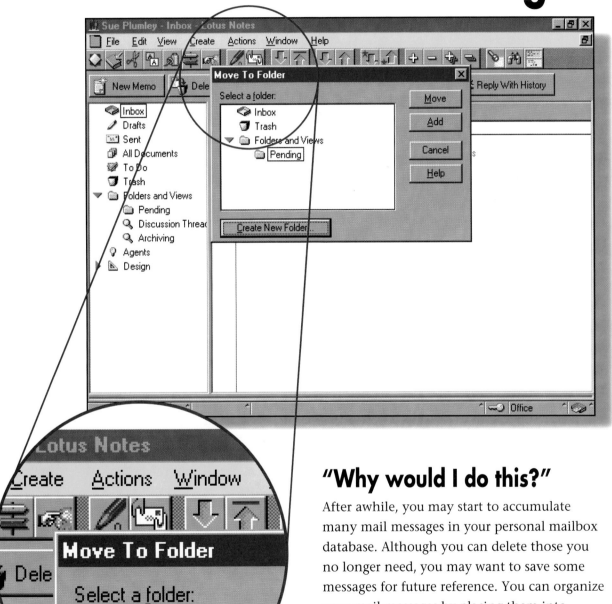

"Why would I do this?"

After awhile, you may start to accumulate many mail messages in your personal mailbox database. Although you can delete those you no longer need, you may want to save some messages for future reference. You can organize your mail messages by placing them into folders. In this lesson, you create a new folder to store messages and move a message to that folder.

1 Open your mail database, and in the Navigation pane, click the **Inbox**. Highlight the message you want to move and click the **Move To Folder** button.

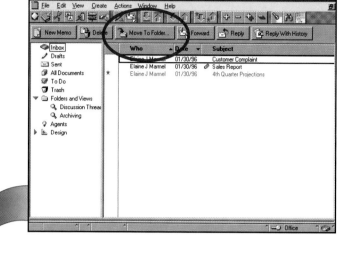

> **NOTE** ▼
>
> You can also move messages in the Sent view, the All Documents view, the Trash view, and the Discussion Thread view.

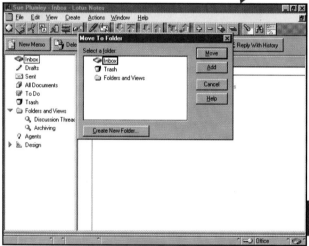

2 Notes displays the Move To Folder dialog box.

3 Choose the **Create New Folder** button to create a new folder.

> **NOTE** ▼
>
> If the folder you want to place the message in already exists, skip to step 5.

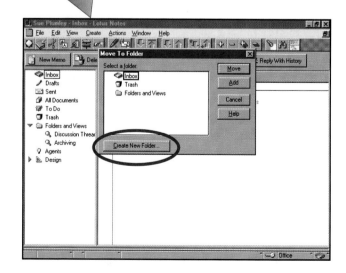

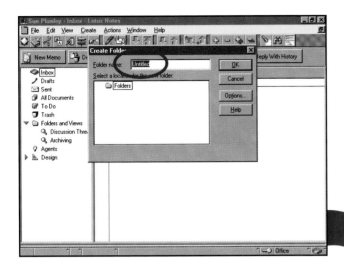

4 Notes displays the Create Folder dialog box. In the Folder name text box, type a name for the new folder (I created "Pending") and choose **OK** to redisplay the Move To Folder dialog box.

5 Highlight the folder in which you want to store the message and choose **Move**.

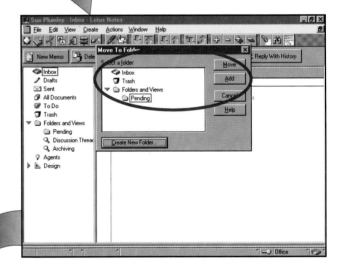

6 Notes closes the dialog box. The message disappears from the Inbox but appears in the folder where you moved it. ■

> **NOTE** ▼
>
> You can move messages to folders while the message is open and you're reading it. Simply open the message and complete steps 2–5.

Deleting Mail

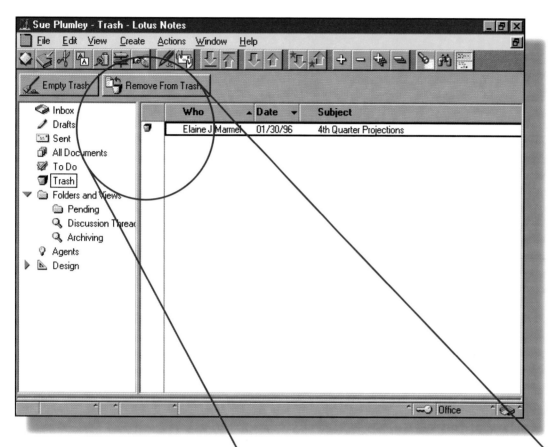

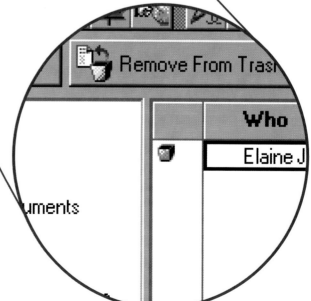

"Why would I do this?"

You can delete mail messages you no longer need in two ways: either while you read the message or from one of the views where you see the message's subject. Regardless of which method you use, you initially mark messages for deletion; you'll see a trash can icon appear next to a marked message. After marking for deletion, you must take a second action: refresh the view to actually delete the messages you marked.

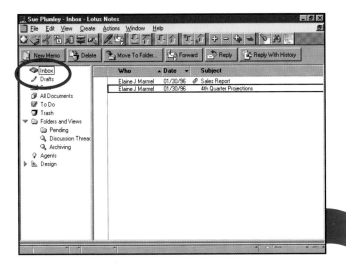

1 Open the mail database and select the view containing messages you want to delete.

2 Highlight the message you want to delete and click the **Delete** button. Notes marks the message for deletion by displaying a trash can next to the message. Repeat this step for each message you want to delete.

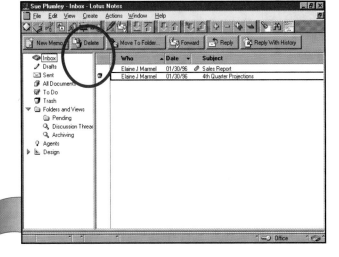

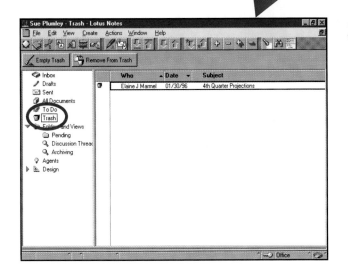

3 Select the **Trash** view. Click the **Empty Trash** button to delete documents, or highlight a particular document and click the **Remove From Trash** button to avoid deleting the document. ■

Replying to a Message

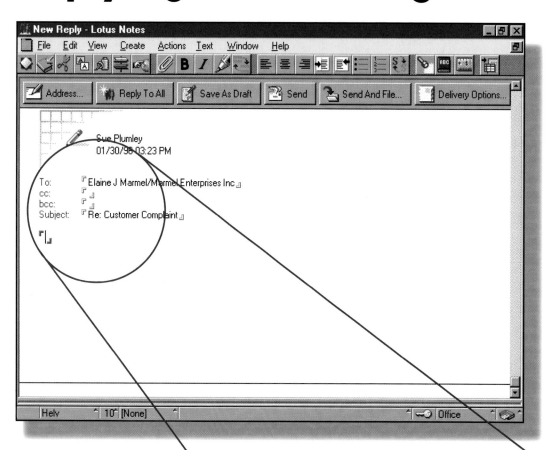

"Why would I do this?"

"Mail" usually implies a two-way correspondence. While you aren't required to answer mail messages, you'll have many occasions where you want to respond to the sender. In Notes, you use the Reply feature to answer a message.

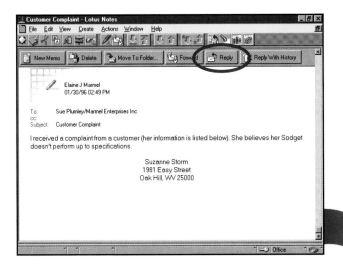

1 Open your mail database and open the message to which you want to reply. Click the **Reply** button.

WHY WORRY?

If someone responds to a message you send and you open the response, you'll see an icon next to the subject that represents the original message. You can double-click that icon to open your original message.

2 Notes opens a new screen that contains the address of the person who originally sent you the message and the subject of the message.

WHY WORRY?

If you want to include the original text in the reply, click the Reply with History. Notes incorporates the text of the memo to which you are replying in the reply.

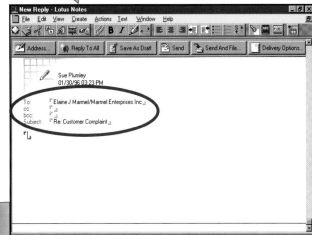

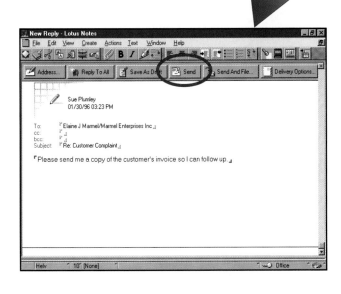

3 Fill in the message and click the **Send** button. ■

NOTE ▼

If you want to keep a copy of the message, choose Send and File.

Forwarding a Message

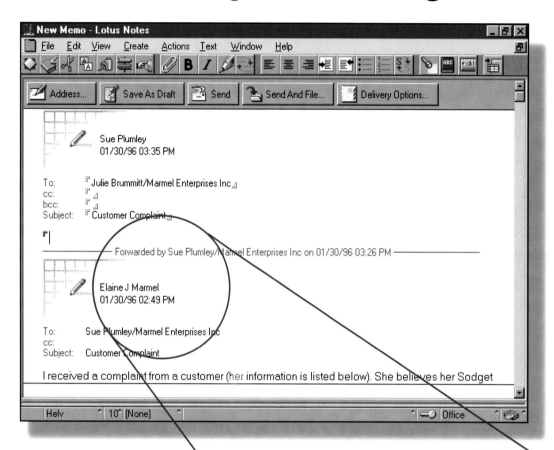

"Why would I do this?"

You may receive a mail message that you want to pass along to someone else. In Notes, you forward the message. You can forward any message in any database to another Notes user. And, you can forward the message while reading it or from any of these views: the Inbox view, the Sent view, the All Documents view, the Discussion Thread view, and any of the folders you create.

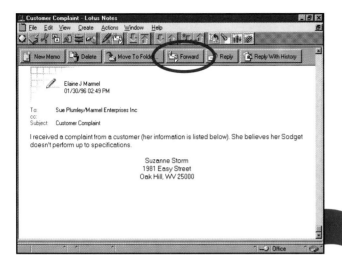

1 Open your mail database and open the message you want to forward. Click the **Forward** button.

NOTE ▼

You can also forward messages without opening them; select the view containing the message you want to forward.

2 Notes redraws your screen and creates a copy of the message, waiting for you to supply a recipient. The top portion of the screen shows you as the sender, and the bottom portion of the screen shows who sent you the message that you are forwarding.

WHY WORRY?

If you're unsure about addressing a message, use the Address Book. You'll learn more about it in a moment.

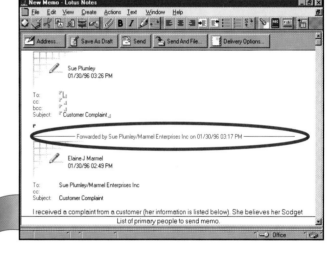

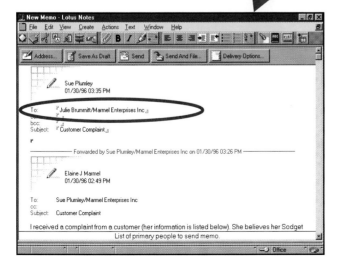

3 Type the recipient's address in the To field. Be sure to include their mail address and their domain name, separated by the forward slash (/). Click the **Send** button to forward the message. Notes sends the message and redisplays the original. ■

NOTE ▼

If you want to keep a copy of the message, choose Send and File.

Adding Entries to Your Address Book

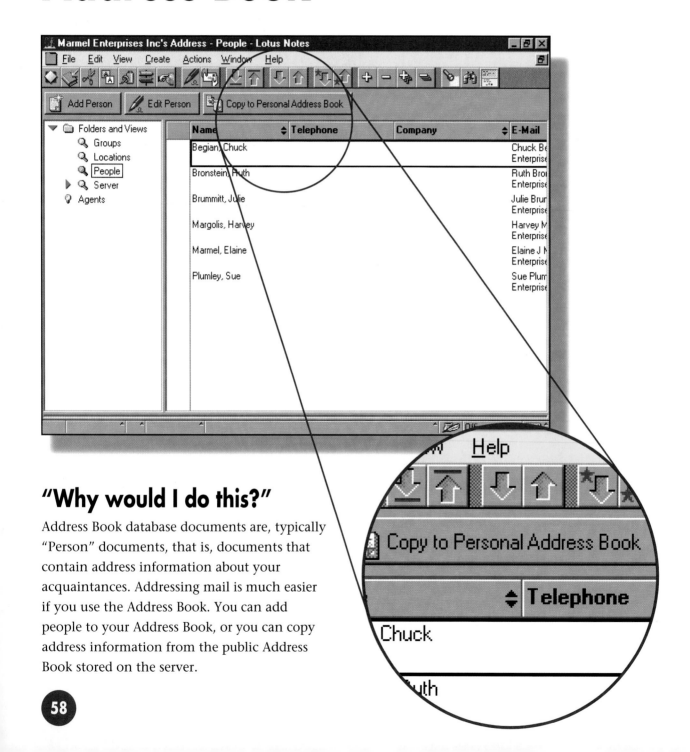

"Why would I do this?"

Address Book database documents are, typically "Person" documents, that is, documents that contain address information about your acquaintances. Addressing mail is much easier if you use the Address Book. You can add people to your Address Book, or you can copy address information from the public Address Book stored on the server.

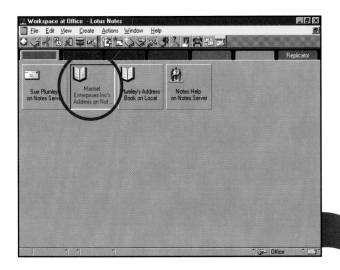

1 From the Workspace tab, open the public Address Book database. It's the Address Book icon that doesn't contain your name.

2 Highlight the name of the person whose address information you want to place in your own Address Book database, and click **Copy to Personal Address Book**.

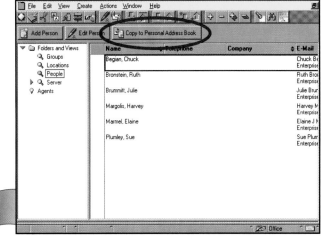

NOTE ▼

You can copy multiple addresses simultaneously by selecting several names. Highlight a name and click or press the Spacebar; you'll see a check next to the name. Repeat this action to select additional names.

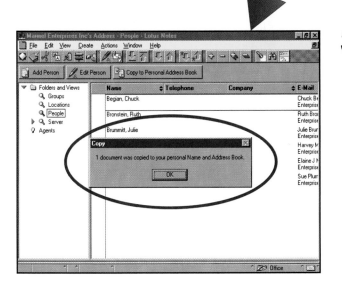

3 Notes displays the message that one document was copied to your personal Address Book.

4 Open the **File** menu and choose the **Close** command to close the server's Address Book database and return to the Workspace pages. Open your personal Address Book database—the one with your name on it.

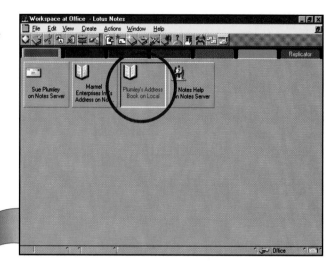

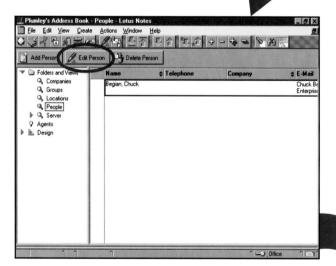

5 You'll see the name(s) and address(es) you copied in the People view of your personal address book. Highlight a name and click the **Edit Person** button.

WHY WORRY?

If this is the first time you opened your Address Book, you will see the About This Database page for the Address Book. Open the File menu and choose Close.

6 Notes displays a Person document; you can use this document as a model if you want to manually add a person to your local Address Book database. ∎

NOTE ▼

To manually add a person to your local Address Book database, open that database, click Add Person, and fill out the Person document.

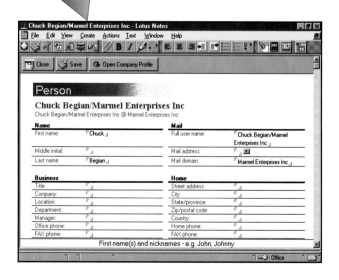

Creating a New Message

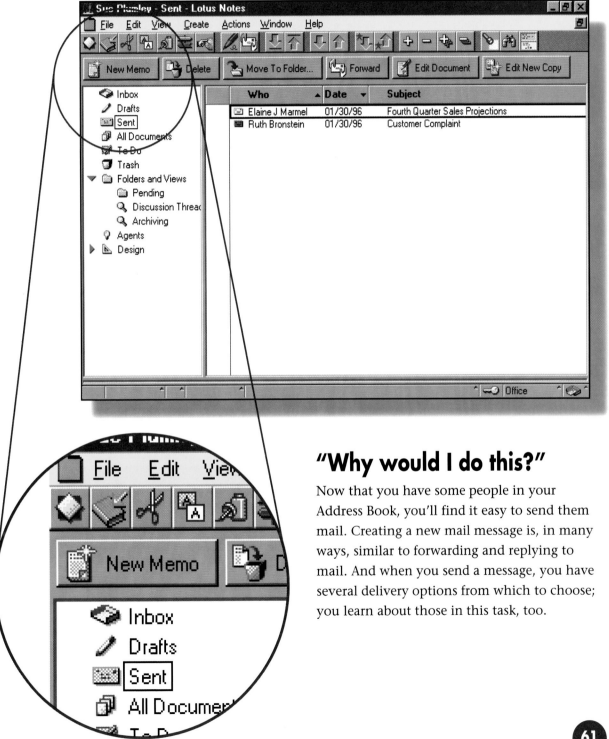

"Why would I do this?"

Now that you have some people in your Address Book, you'll find it easy to send them mail. Creating a new mail message is, in many ways, similar to forwarding and replying to mail. And when you send a message, you have several delivery options from which to choose; you learn about those in this task, too.

1 Open your Mail database and click the **New Memo** button.

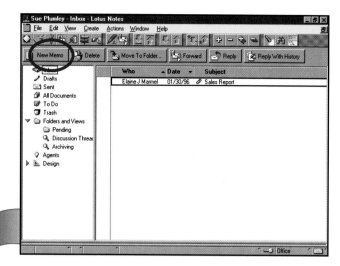

2 Notes displays a new memo ready for you to complete. Click the **Address** button to select a name from the Address book.

3 From the list on the left, select the person to whom you want to send the mail. Then, click the **To:>** button.

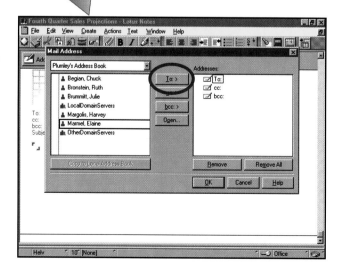

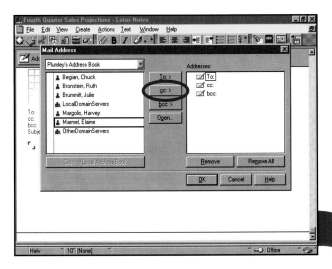

4 (Optional) To send a carbon copy of the message, select a person from the list on the left and click the **cc:>** button.

5 When you have finished choosing the people to whom you want to send your message, your selections are shown in the list on the right. Choose **OK**.

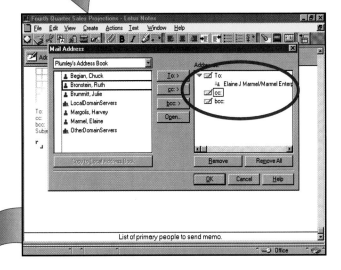

List of primary people to send memo.

6 Notes fills in the address portion of the new mail message.

List of people to send a copy of the memo.

7 Fill in the subject line and the message. Then, click the **Delivery Options** button. See the table at the end of this task for an explanation of the Delivery options.

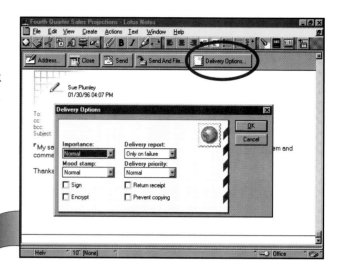

WHY WORRY?

If you don't see any envelopes in the Sent view, Notes may not be set up to keep copies of mail you send. In Customizing the Notes workspace, you'll learn how to set this option.

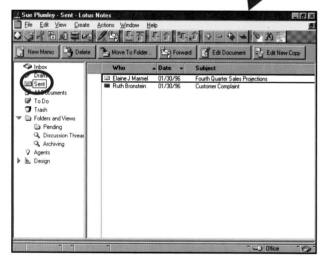

8 Select your Delivery options and choose **OK**. Notes redisplays your message. Click **Send** to close and send the message. Click the **Sent** view to see your message. A red envelope will appear if you set a priority other than Normal. A yellow envelope will appear if you didn't change the message's priority. ■

Delivery Option	Description
Importance	Displays an icon to the recipient that illustrates how important the memo is.
Mood stamp	Personalize the message with options such as Personal, Confidential, Private, and Thank You.
Delivery report	Requests a confirmation that Notes has delivered your message. Only on Failure sends a report only if the server failed to deliver the message; Confirm Delivery sends a message confirming delivery or reporting failure; Trace Entire Path sends reports from every server through which the message is routed.
Delivery priority	High routes the message immediately; Normal routes the message the next time the server is scheduled to send mail; Low routes the message during off-peak hours, usually between midnight and 6 a.m.
Sign	Incorporates a digital signature in your message, assuring the recipient that you are, indeed, the person who sent the message.
Encrypt	Makes a message readable to the recipient only.
Return receipt	Requests a confirmation that your message has been read by the recipient.
Prevent copying	Sends a message that the recipient cannot forward.

Attaching a Document to a Mail Message

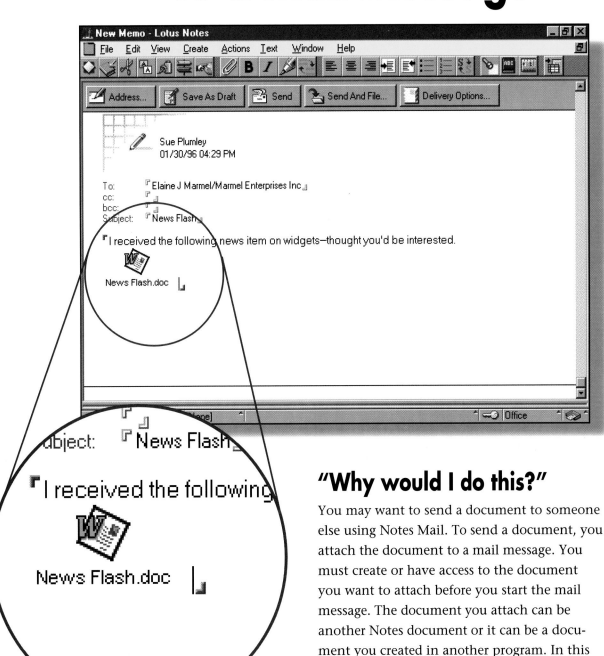

"Why would I do this?"

You may want to send a document to someone else using Notes Mail. To send a document, you attach the document to a mail message. You must create or have access to the document you want to attach before you start the mail message. The document you attach can be another Notes document or it can be a document you created in another program. In this task, you learn how to attach a News Flash already created in Microsoft Word.

1 Open your Mail database and click the **New Memo** button.

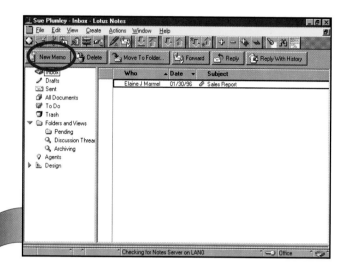

2 Notes displays a new memo ready for you to complete. Click the **Address** button to open the Address Book.

3 Select an addressee and choose **OK**.

NOTE ▼

If you type a few letters of the person's last name, Notes will display the Quick Search dialog box and search for the letters you type.

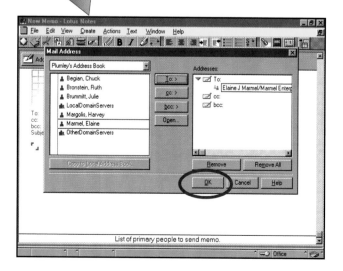

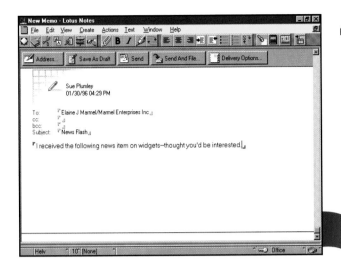

4 Notes fills in the address information. Complete the subject and type any text you want to include in the mail message. Optionally, press **Enter** to start a new line before attaching the document.

5 Open the **File** menu and choose the **Attach** command. Notes displays the Create Attachment(s) dialog box. Navigate to the folder containing the document you want to attach, highlight the document, and choose **Create**.

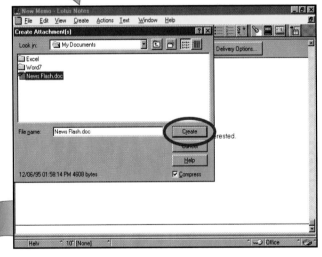

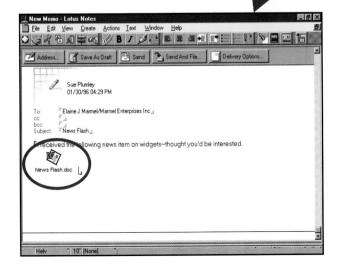

6 Notes inserts an attachment icon in your message. The icon you see depends on the type of document you chose to detach. ■

Creating a Mailing List

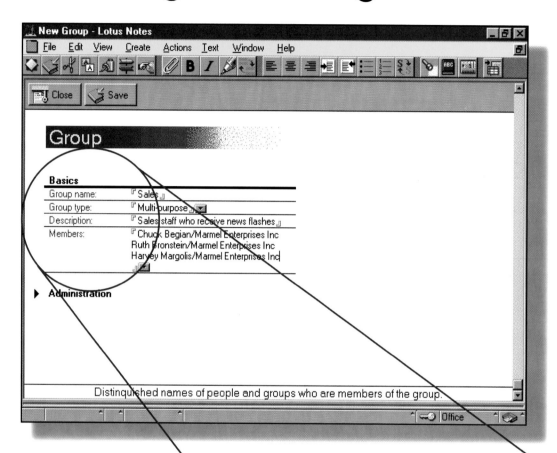

"Why would I do this?"

You may find that you regularly send mail to the same group of people. Instead of selecting them individually each time you need to send them mail, you can create a mailing list in your personal Address Book database that includes them and simply select the list. Notes will then send the message to each person included in the list.

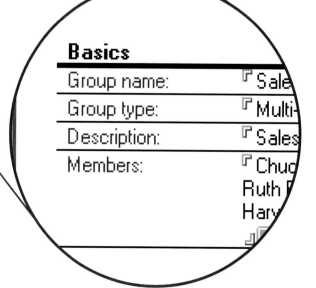

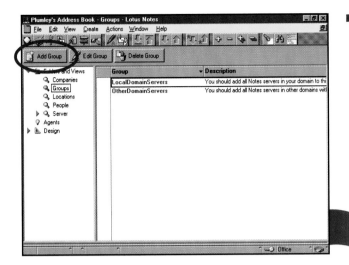

1 Open your personal Address Book and, in the Navigation pane, click **Groups**. Click the **Add Group** button.

2 Notes displays a Group document.

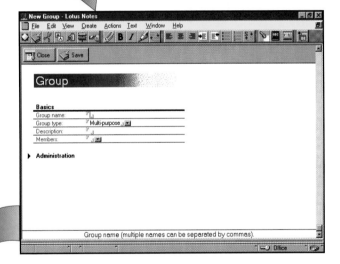

3 Next to Group name, type the name you want to use when addressing the group. You'll find it most useful to use a name that describes the group or its purpose. For example, you could name the group Sales if the group contains members of the Sales department. Leave the Group type as Multi-purpose and supply, if you want, a description of the group.

4 Click the down arrow next to members to open the Names dialog box.

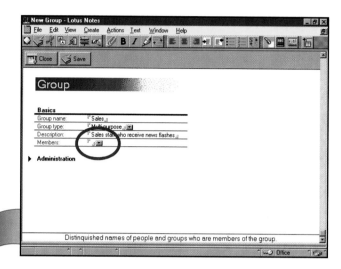

5 From the list box on the left side of the Names dialog box, highlight a name and click **Add>**.

6 Repeat step 5 to add each person you want to include in the Group.

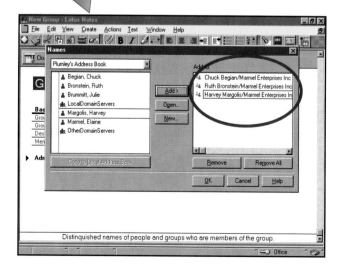

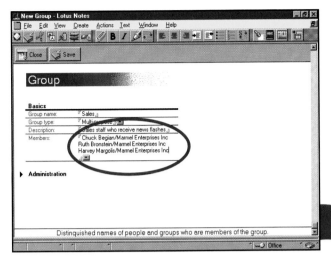

7 Click **OK** to insert the names into the Group document.

8 Click the **File Save** SmartIcon, or open the **File** menu and choose **Save** to save the Group document.

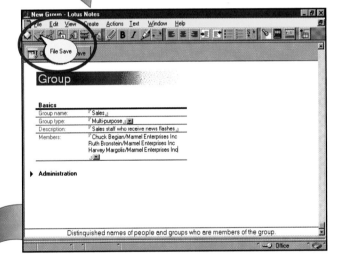

9 Close the Group document, which now appears in your personal Address Book when you select **Group** from the Navigation pane. ∎

Sending Mail to a Group of People

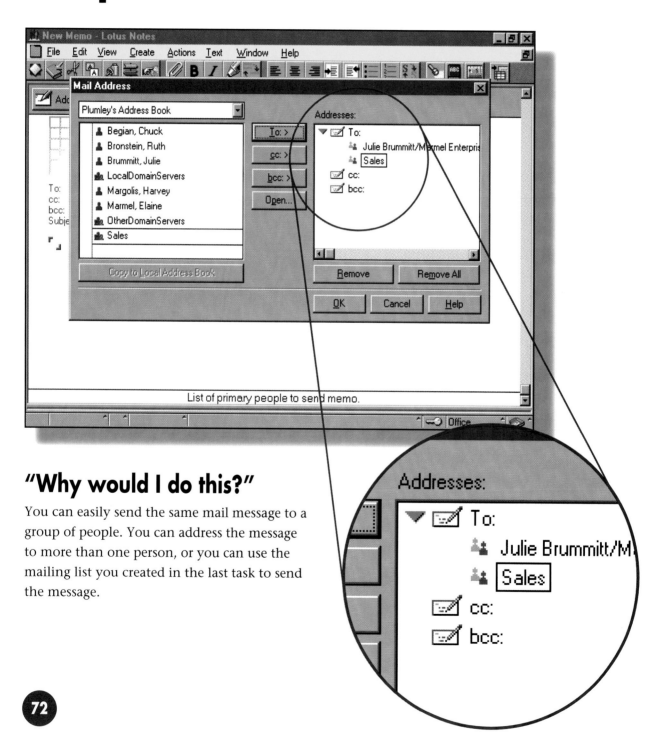

"Why would I do this?"

You can easily send the same mail message to a group of people. You can address the message to more than one person, or you can use the mailing list you created in the last task to send the message.

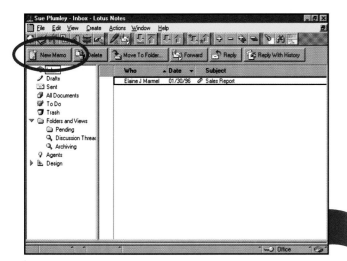

1 Open your mail database, and click the **New Memo** button to start creating a new mail message.

2 Click the **Address** button to open your address book.

To use your mailing list, highlight it and click the To:> button.

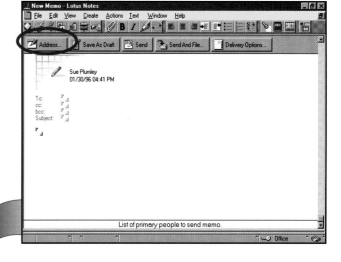

3 Highlight the first name to whom you want to send the message and click the **To:>** button. Repeat this action for each person to whom you want to send the message. When you choose OK, the name of each person you selected will appear in the To section of your mail message, and Notes will deliver a copy of the message to each of them. ■

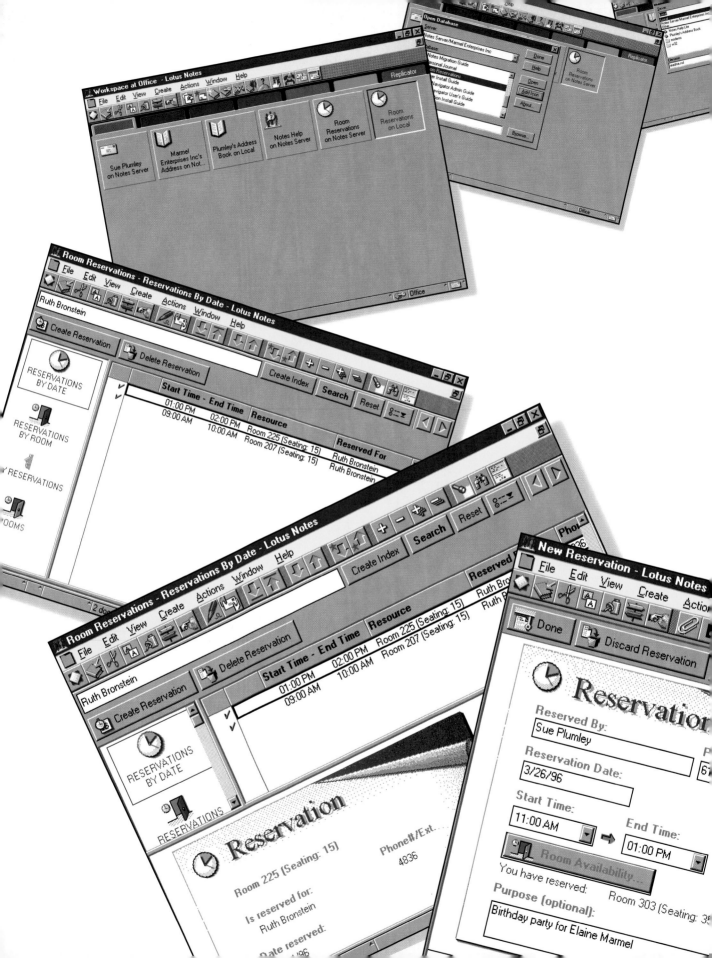

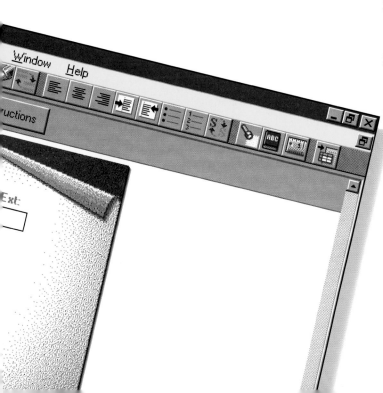

PART III

Using Notes Databases and Documents

When you use Lotus Notes, you work in one of several databases. Again, remember that Notes uses the term *database* to compartmentalize information in a single area of interest that you might want to share. Notes databases, therefore, are not necessarily like the traditional database you think of when you hear the term database. For example, when you use mail in Notes, you are using at least one Notes database—the Mail database. And, as you saw in Part II, you might also use the Address Book database in conjunction with the Mail database when you send mail.

When Notes is installed, your Mail database is created. You'll find some other databases out there that came with Notes, such as the Help files. But most of the databases you use in Notes are created by someone in your company—and that person could be you. You'll learn more about creating databases in Part IV. In Part III, you'll learn how to use an existing database. Throughout most of this part, I'll use, as the example database, a Room Reservation database that I built. In this database, you can reserve rooms for use on specific dates at specific times. While you won't find the exact database I'm using, you may find a similar database on your Notes system. But, if not, don't worry; you can perform the tasks described in this part on almost any database you find on your system. You might want to check with your administrator to get the name of a database for which you have privileges.

Notes databases reside on a server so that everyone using Notes can access the database. In "Adding a Database to Your Workspace," you'll create an icon that helps you easily open and close the database on the server. Adding databases can be tricky because you need to know the network server on which they are stored before you can add them to your workspace. Don't worry; you will soon become familiar enough with your Notes network to easily navigate it and find the databases you need. And, in the meantime, your network administrator can help you by supplying a path to Notes databases which you can access.

After you learn how to open and close a database on the server, you'll learn how to create a copy of the database that you can use on your own computer instead of using the database on the server. The copy you create is a "local copy" and when you use it, you're "working locally." When you work locally, you can make changes to the database while you are not connected to the server. This is particularly useful when a database contains information you use regularly and you want to keep a copy of that information on your own computer so that you can use it even if the server is down.

Whether you use the Mail database, the Room Reservation database, or another database, certain commands work consistently. For example, you can open, close, copy, remove, and add all databases on your workspace in the same way. You also use the same technique to open and close documents in each database—as you learned in Part II, you either double-click the document or highlight it and choose an appropriate button (Open or Edit) from the action bar. This consistency across databases makes it easy to use and share any database on the system.

While some features are the same across databases, each database also has its own unique characteristics as well, because each database has its own set of documents. For example, different databases may have different buttons at the top in the action bar to reflect the actions available. In the Room Reservation database that you'll see in the tasks coming up, you cannot open documents (reservations) to edit them or read them because of the design of the database. Instead, you can only create or delete reservations. In this way, the Room Reservation database is unique. So, unlike your Mail database, you won't see a button on the action bar in the Room Reservation database to open or edit documents.

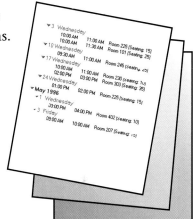

Typically, while you work in a database, you want to search for documents instead of reading every document in the database. The designer of the database usually builds a *full text index*, which is a list of words found in the database for you so that you can quickly search through the database for documents that interest you.

Because you may want to preview a document to see if it is one you want to open or print, you'll learn how to preview documents in Part III. And, using the Room Reservation database, you'll learn how to add a document to a database. You can add documents to databases only if your privileges in that database allow it; you may need to check with the database designer to obtain these privileges.

Just as different databases have different buttons available in the action bar, different databases also contain different views to see the titles of the documents. You use these views to help you organize the documents in the database. For example, you can organize your Address Book database so that documents (names and addresses) for companies appear in the Companies view, while documents for individuals appear in the People view. In the Room Reservation database, you would most likely want to see reservations organized either by date or by room reserved. So, the Room Reservation database has a Reservations by Date view and a Reservations by Room view.

At the end of Part III, you'll learn about views. You'll learn how to switch views so that you see the documents in the database from a different perspective. And, you'll learn how to print documents from the view (without opening them) as well as how to print the view. And, finally, you'll learn how to remove a database from your workspace once you finish working with the database.

Searching for Databases on the Server

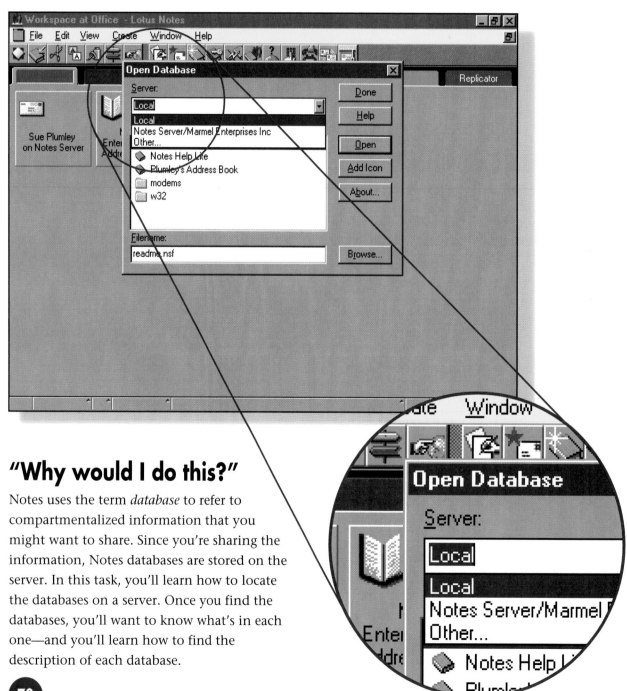

"Why would I do this?"

Notes uses the term *database* to refer to compartmentalized information that you might want to share. Since you're sharing the information, Notes databases are stored on the server. In this task, you'll learn how to locate the databases on a server. Once you find the databases, you'll want to know what's in each one—and you'll learn how to find the description of each database.

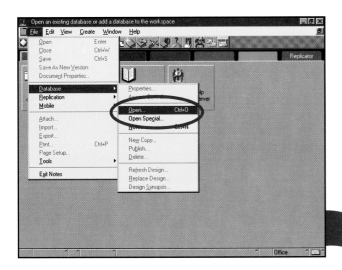

1 Open the **File** menu and choose the **Database** command. From the submenu, choose **Open**. The Open Database dialog box appears.

WHY WORRY?

You may be prompted for your password for your server. If you don't know it, talk to your Notes administrator.

2 Open the Server list box to identify available Servers and choose one.

NOTE ▼

When you find a database you're interested in, you can open it by choosing the Open button in the Open Database dialog box.

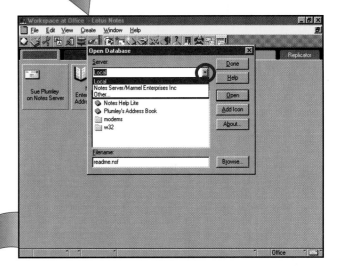

3 To identify the contents and purpose of a database, highlight the database in the Database list and choose About. Notes displays the About This Database page for the highlighted database, which you can read by using the scroll bar at the right of the window. When you finish reading the database description, choose **Close** to redisplay the Open Database dialog box. Then, choose **Done** to close that dialog box. ■

Adding a Database to Your Workspace

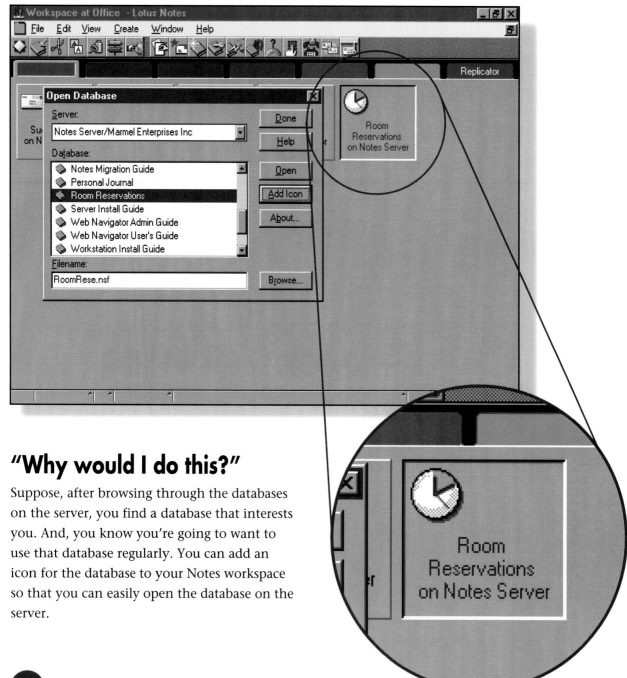

"Why would I do this?"

Suppose, after browsing through the databases on the server, you find a database that interests you. And, you know you're going to want to use that database regularly. You can add an icon for the database to your Notes workspace so that you can easily open the database on the server.

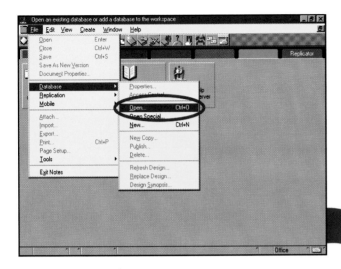

1 Open the **File** menu and choose the **Database** command. From the submenu, choose **Open**. The Open Database dialog box appears.

2 Open the Server list box to identify available Servers and choose one.

WHY WORRY?

You may be prompted for your password for your server. If you don't know it, talk to your Notes administrator.

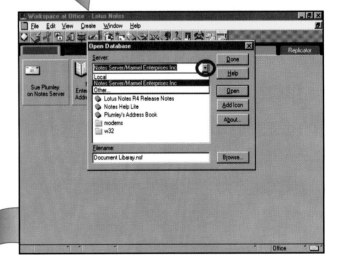

3 Highlight the database you want to add to your workspace and click the **Add Icon** button. The icon for the database appears on your workspace. Click **Done** to close the Open Database dialog box. ▇

Copying a Database to Your Local Machine

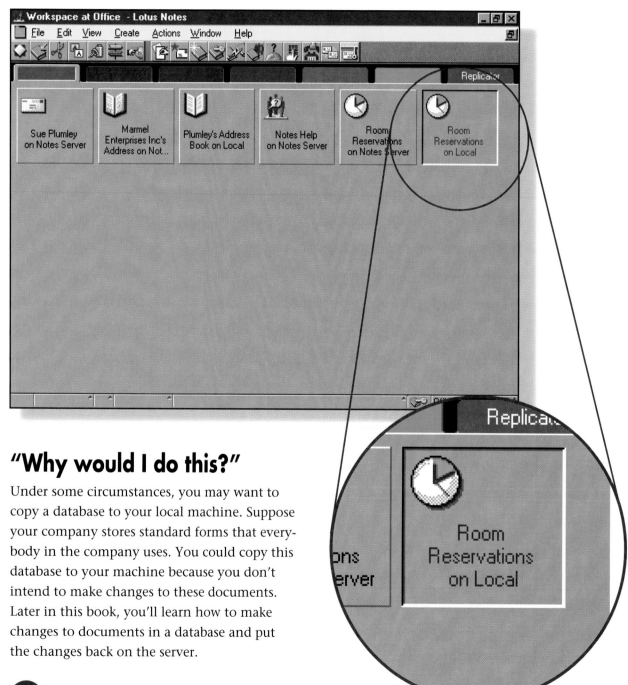

"Why would I do this?"

Under some circumstances, you may want to copy a database to your local machine. Suppose your company stores standard forms that everybody in the company uses. You could copy this database to your machine because you don't intend to make changes to these documents. Later in this book, you'll learn how to make changes to documents in a database and put the changes back on the server.

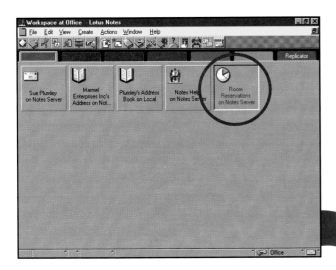

1 If you haven't already added an icon for the database you want to copy to your workspace, do so following the steps in the last task. Click the icon for the database once to select the database.

2 Open the **File** menu and choose **Database**. From the submenu, choose **New Copy**.

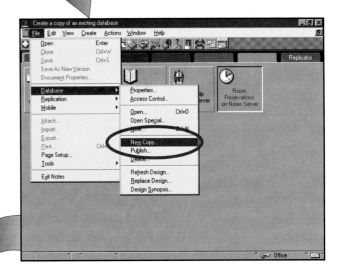

3 Make sure Local appears in the Server list box. If you want to change the title of the database, change it in the Title text box.

4 Remove the check from the Access Control List to ensure you have access to the database after you copy it.

> **NOTE** ▼
>
> To later search this database quickly, check Create Full Text index. Notes may tell you that this is a local database and must be indexed manually, but Notes will also ask if you want to index the database now. Choose Yes.

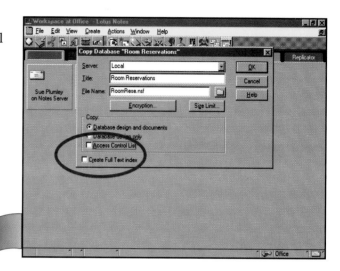

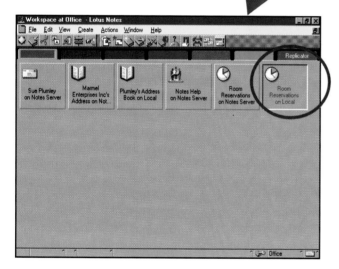

5 Choose **OK**. Notes copies the database to your computer. A new icon appears on your workspace tab containing the database name and the words on `Local`. ▨

> **NOTE** ▼
>
> You can work in this database even if the server is not operating. If you make changes to the local copy, you can update the database on the server with your changes by *replicating* (see Part V for more about how to replicate a database).

TASK 28
Searching for Text

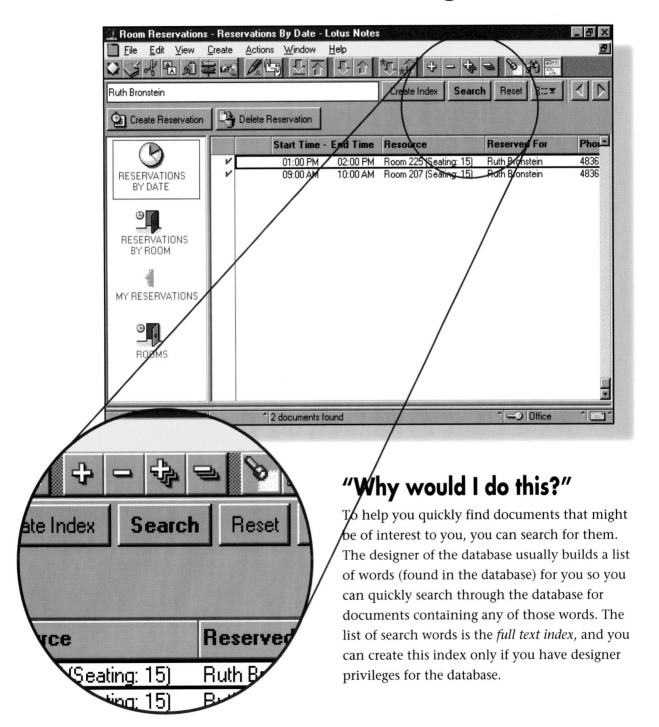

"Why would I do this?"

To help you quickly find documents that might be of interest to you, you can search for them. The designer of the database usually builds a list of words (found in the database) for you so you can quickly search through the database for documents containing any of those words. The list of search words is the *full text index*, and you can create this index only if you have designer privileges for the database.

85

1 Open the database you want to search.

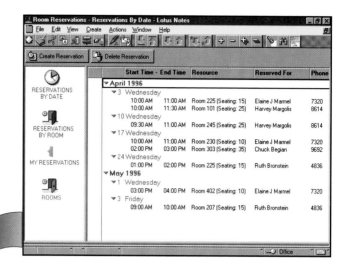

WHY WORRY?

If this is the first time you have opened this database, you may see the About This Database document. Press Esc or choose File Close to close the document.

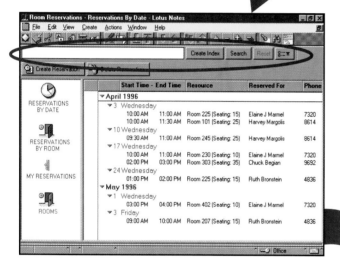

2 Open the **View** menu and choose **Search Bar** to display the Search bar above the action bar.

WHY WORRY?

To redisplay all documents, click the Reset button in the Search bar. To close the Search bar, reopen the View menu and choose Search Bar again.

3 Click in the text box in the Search bar and type the characters for which you want to search. Click the **Search** button, and Notes displays the documents found that match what you typed. ■

NOTE ▼

The more characters you type, the fewer matches Notes is likely to find.

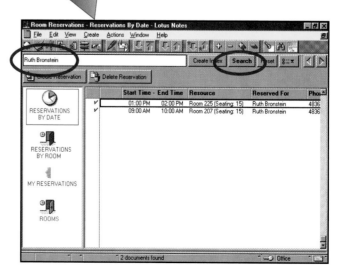

Previewing a Document

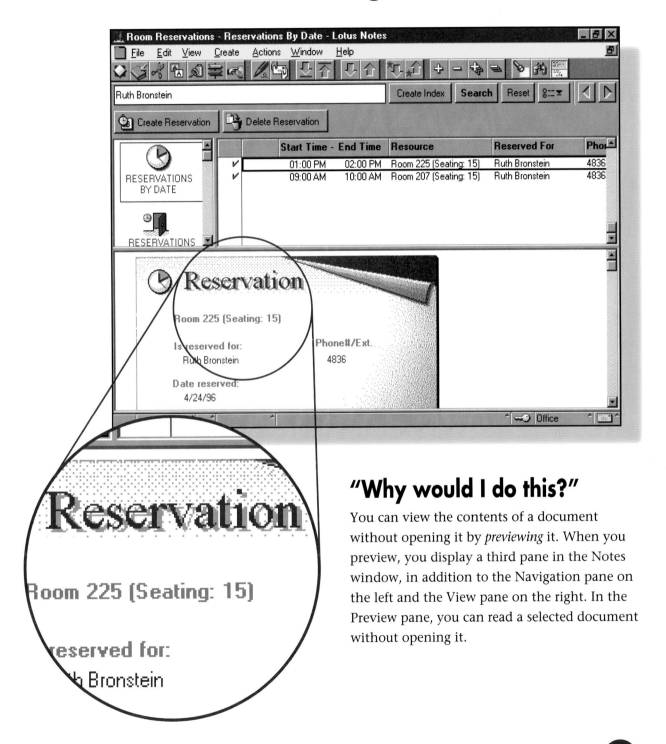

"Why would I do this?"

You can view the contents of a document without opening it by *previewing* it. When you preview, you display a third pane in the Notes window, in addition to the Navigation pane on the left and the View pane on the right. In the Preview pane, you can read a selected document without opening it.

1 Open a database and highlight a document you want to preview. Use one of the documents found in the search in the last task.

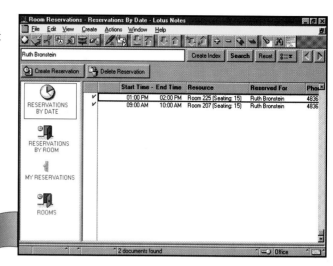

2 Open the **View** menu and choose **Document Preview**.

WHY WORRY?

To close the Preview pane, open the View menu again and choose Document Preview again.

3 Notes opens a Preview pane at the bottom of the screen and displays the contents of the highlighted document. If you can't see all of the document, use the scroll bar at the right edge of the screen. ■

NOTE ▼

To preview a different document, click that document to select it. Notes changes the contents of the Preview pane.

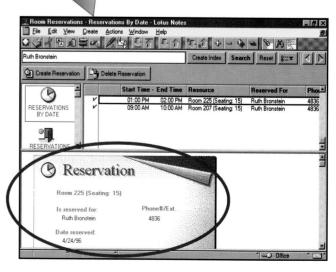

Adding a Document to a Database

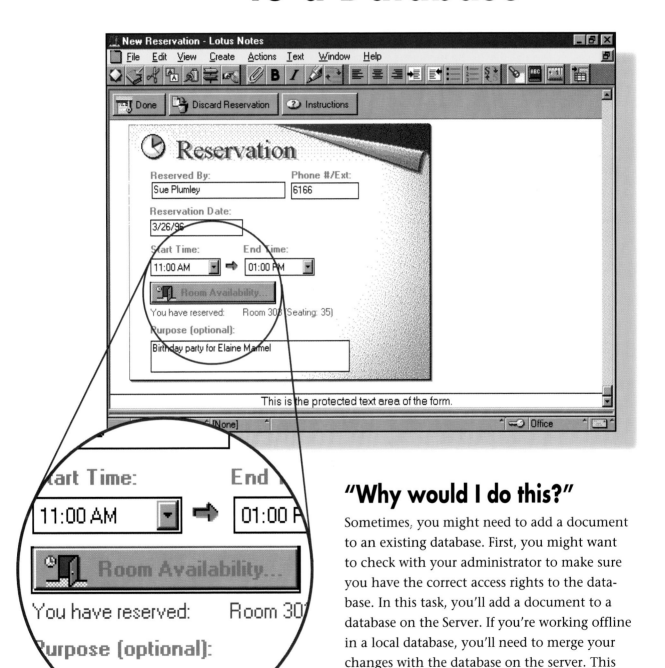

"Why would I do this?"

Sometimes, you might need to add a document to an existing database. First, you might want to check with your administrator to make sure you have the correct access rights to the database. In this task, you'll add a document to a database on the Server. If you're working offline in a local database, you'll need to merge your changes with the database on the server. This process is called *replicating* and you'll learn how to replicate in Part V.

1 On the action bar, you should see a button you can click to create a new document. In the Mail database, you saw the New Memo button. In the Address Book database, you saw the Add Person button. The button you see depends on the database and view at which you are looking. In the Room Reservation database, the button is Create Reservation.

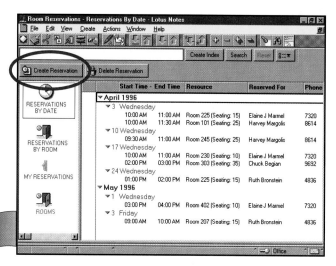

2 When you click the button, Notes displays a form you can complete. When you finish the form, save and close the document. In the Reservation database, choose the **Done** button. In the Address Book database, use the **Save** and **Close** buttons or open the **File** menu and choose the **Save** command. Then, open the **File** menu and choose the **Close** command.

3 When Notes redisplays the Navigation and View panes, you'll see the document you created. ▪

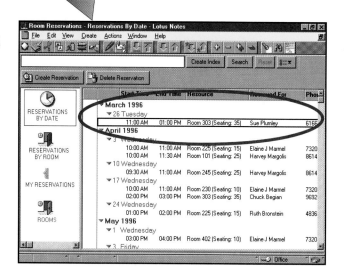

NOTE ▼

Typically, the action bar contains a button you can click to finish. In the Room Reservations database, you can click Done to both save and close the reservation.

Changing Views

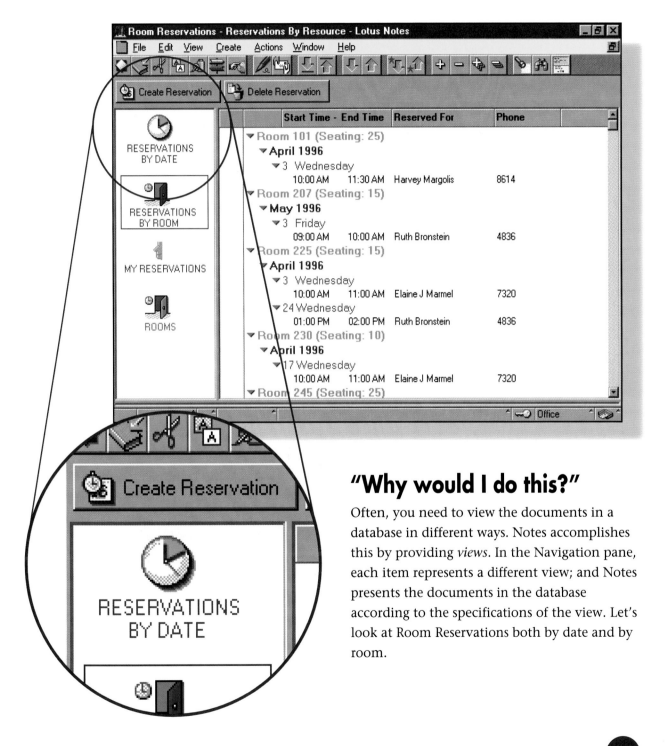

"Why would I do this?"

Often, you need to view the documents in a database in different ways. Notes accomplishes this by providing *views*. In the Navigation pane, each item represents a different view; and Notes presents the documents in the database according to the specifications of the view. Let's look at Room Reservations both by date and by room.

1 Make sure both the Preview pane and the Search bar are closed by deselecting them.

NOTE ▼

Open the View menu and, if checks appear next to either Search Bar or Document Preview, choose the command to remove the check mark and close the Search Bar or the Document Preview window.

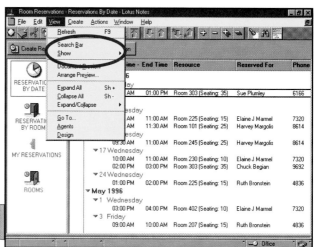

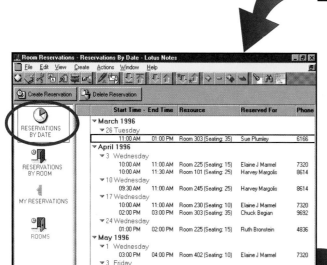

2 In the Navigation pane, click on the view you want to see. Click on Reservations by Date, and Notes displays all reservations ordered by date.

3 In the Navigation pane, click on another view you want to see. Click on Reservations by Room, and Notes displays all reservations ordered by room. ■

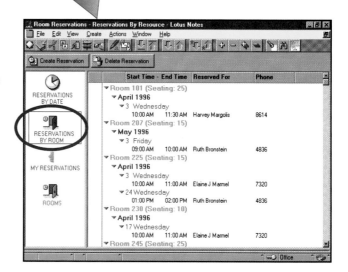

Printing Documents from a View

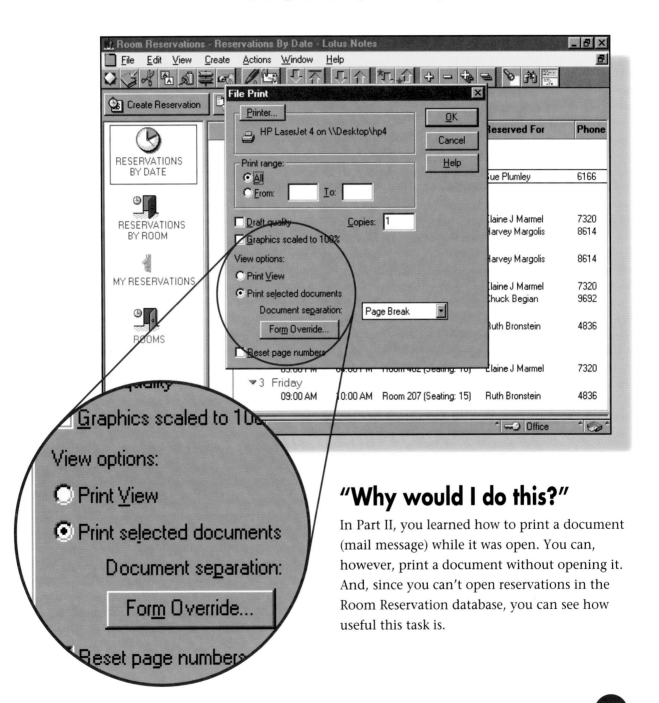

"Why would I do this?"

In Part II, you learned how to print a document (mail message) while it was open. You can, however, print a document without opening it. And, since you can't open reservations in the Room Reservation database, you can see how useful this task is.

1 Highlight the document you want to print. If you want to print more than one document, select each by clicking in the column to the left of the document or by pressing the Spacebar after highlighting to place a check next to the document.

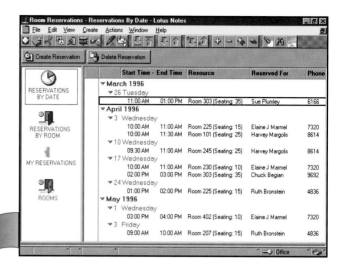

2 Press the *right* mouse button to display a shortcut menu. Select the **Print** command and the File Print dialog box appears.

3 Leave the settings in the Print dialog box set to print the selected documents and choose **OK**. Notes prints the contents of the selected documents. ■

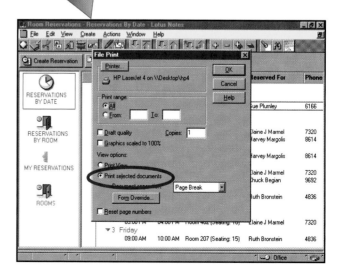

Printing a View

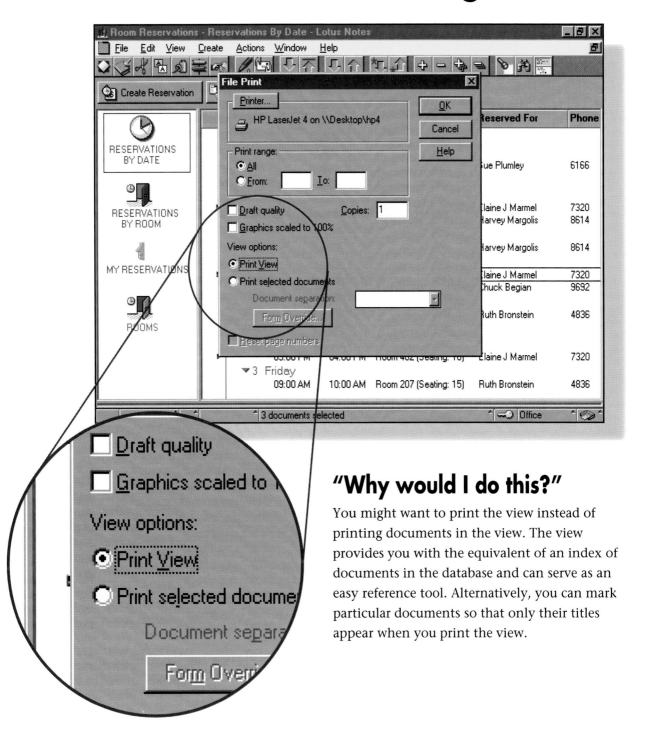

"Why would I do this?"

You might want to print the view instead of printing documents in the view. The view provides you with the equivalent of an index of documents in the database and can serve as an easy reference tool. Alternatively, you can mark particular documents so that only their titles appear when you print the view.

1 Select the view you want to print and display the documents you want to print.

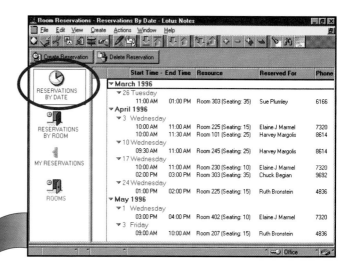

NOTE ▼

If you don't select any documents, Notes prints the titles of all documents in the view. If you *do* select documents, Notes prints the titles of only the selected documents.

2 (Optional) To print the titles of selected documents only, highlight any documents you want to select and press the Spacebar to select them. Notes places a check mark next to them.

WHY WORRY?

When you finish using the database, open the File menu and choose Close to close the database.

3 Open the **File** menu and choose the **Print** command. In the Print dialog box, choose **Print View**. When you choose **OK**, Notes prints a copy of the view to the selected printer. ■

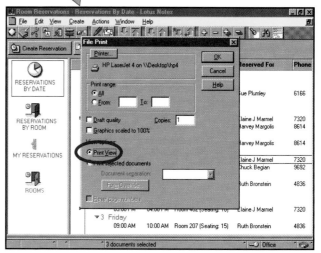

Removing a Database from Your Workspace

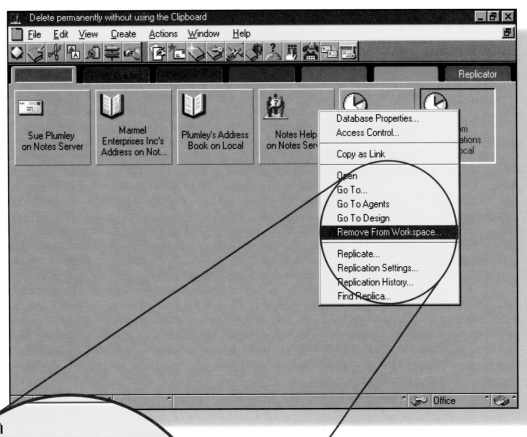

"Why would I do this?"

Once you finish working with a database, you may not want it in your workspace any longer. You can remove the database icon from your workspace. Removing the icon doesn't affect the database or any other Notes user. You simply can't open the database again by clicking on its icon. You can always add the database to your workspace again the same way you did earlier in this part.

1 On the workspace page, point at the icon for the database you want to remove.

WHY WORRY?

You can display the workspace page by clicking the Window Workspace SmartIcon.

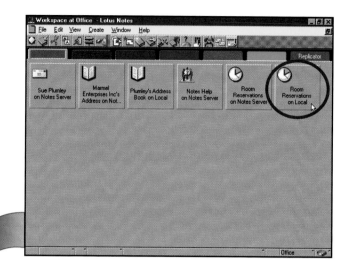

2 Click the *right* mouse button to display a shortcut menu and choose **Remove From Workspace**.

3 Notes displays the dialog box you see in the figure. Choose **Yes**. ■

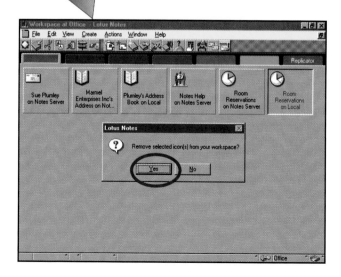

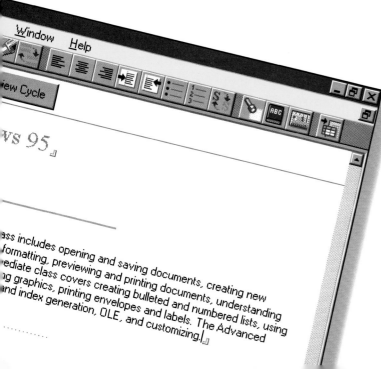

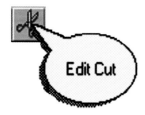

So, now it's time to create your own database—your own compartment that contains information you want to share with others. Perhaps you want to create a database that contains news releases about your company. Or perhaps you're in charge of proposal preparation, and your company's policy is that all proposals must have a consistent look. So, you want to create a database that contains forms your company uses when creating proposals.

When you create a database, you use a template that Notes supplies as the foundation of the database. The template for the database contains default settings such as the views you'll see in the database and the buttons you'll see on the action bar.

The database template also contains some default *forms*. Forms serve as the foundation you use when you create a document. You can think of forms as templates for database documents. The forms also contain default information that Notes uses when you create or edit a document. For example, Notes might supply a drop-down list for a particular field on a document. Notes knows that the field should display the drop-down list because the form contains that information. In this part, you'll learn how to create a new database and create documents in that database, but you won't learn about designing new forms. Instead, you'll use the default forms that appear in the database and create documents based on those forms. Why? Because designing a new form is rather complex and beyond the scope of this book. But don't worry—in most cases, the default forms you'll find in a database are adequate to meet your needs.

As you create documents, you'll learn how to edit. In particular, you'll learn how to select, move, and copy text. And, of course, you'll learn how to undo an action. To enhance text, you'll learn how to apply attributes such as boldface or italics. You'll also set tabs, insert page breaks, create headers and footers, find and replace text, create tables, and check spelling.

Document links (known as *DocLinks* in Notes) provide a way for you to switch a reader from the current document to another document, view, folder, or even database. You can think of DocLinks the same way you think of the attachments to mail messages you learned about in Part II. But, DocLinks differ from attachments in one way: attachments point to files not created in Notes, while DocLinks point to other Notes elements. In this part, you'll learn how to create and use DocLinks.

Hotspots are highlighted text that provide additional information or perform an action when you click them. In Part IV, you'll learn how to create and use a pop-up text hotspot, which provides pop-up text for the reader.

You'll also learn how to *import* data into a Notes document. When you import data, you actually bring information from an outside file into a Notes database. You can import data from spreadsheets or text files. Don't confuse importing with launching an attachment. When you launch an attachment, you use Notes to open the file in its native program. When you import a file, you bring the data in the file into Notes and use the information in Notes.

As you learned in Part III, a database may contain more than one view of your documents; remember the Room Reservation database, where you were able to view documents both by date and by room. Views can be created only by someone who has designer privileges in a database, and views are only one way to organize documents in a database. You also can create categories in a database and assign documents to a category. Then, you can view the documents by category. And, anyone who can view the database and edit the documents can create categories and assign documents to the categories. Again, creating a view is rather complicated and outside the scope of this book, but you will learn, in this part, to create categories and assign documents to those categories. In this part, you'll create a training database similar to one that computer trainers might create (now why doesn't that surprise you?). In the training database, you'll establish and use categories for word processing, spreadsheets, operating systems, and so on.

As the designer of the database, you control who can use your database and what each person can do while working in your database. At the end of this part, you'll learn how to allow others to use a database you create.

Bold

Italic

<u>Underline</u>

TASK 35

Creating a Database

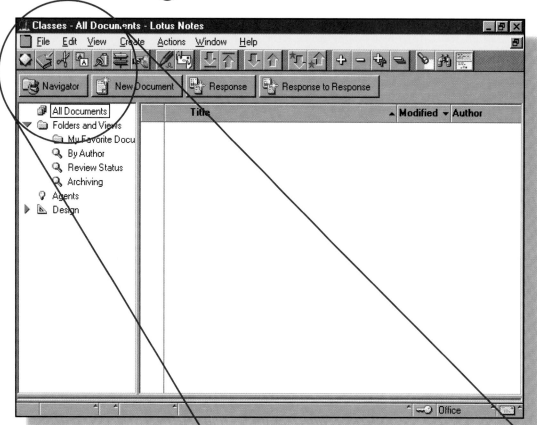

"Why would I do this?"

The easiest way to create a new database is to use one of the templates supplied with Notes as the model for your database. The template contains predefined forms and views as well as other Notes database elements. When you create a database, you want to work on your computer as opposed to a server, so you create the database on your local machine.

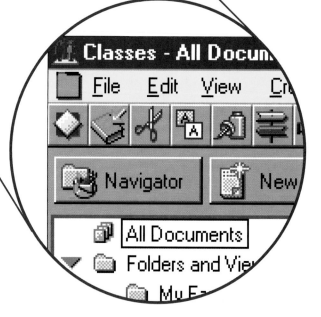

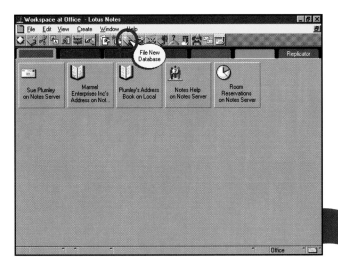

1 Choose the **File New Database** SmartIcon, or open the **File** menu and choose **Database**. From the submenu, choose **New**. Notes displays the New Database dialog box.

2 You want the Server to be Local, so you don't need to make any changes to the Server list box. In the Title text box, type the name for your new database, for example Classes. As you type the database name, Notes assigns it a file name.

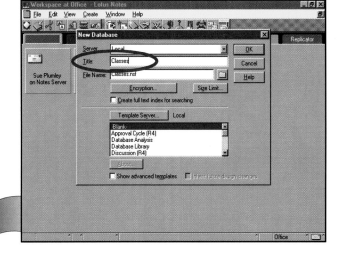

NOTE ▼

The designer of the database usually builds a list of words found in the database so that you can quickly search the database for documents that interest you. The list of search words is the *full text index*.

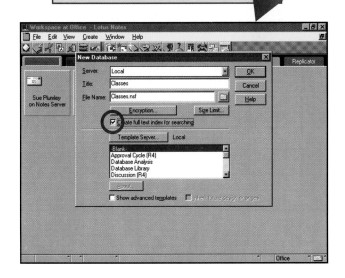

3 Place a check in the **Create full text index for searching** check box. That way, Notes will automatically create the index for your new database.

105

4 (Optional) In the bottom portion of the dialog box, you see a list of database templates available on your computer; notice that the Template Server is set to Local. If you don't see the template you want to use as the basis for your database, click the **Template Server** command button and change to the server containing the templates you want to use. In this example, use the Document Library template.

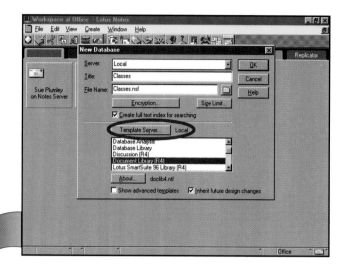

5 Choose **OK**. Notes creates the database, places an icon for it on the current workspace tab, and displays a dialog box that gives you the choice of indexing your database now. When you choose **Yes**, Notes indexes the database. Briefly, on-screen, you see the workspace tab with the icon for your new database. Then, Notes displays the About This Database document.

6 Press **Esc** to close the About This Database document and display your new database. ■

WHY WORRY?

To learn the purpose of any database template, highlight that template in the list, and click the About button. Notes displays the about database document for the template.

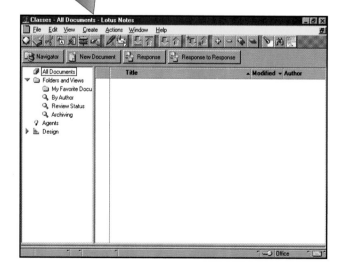

Creating and Saving a New Document

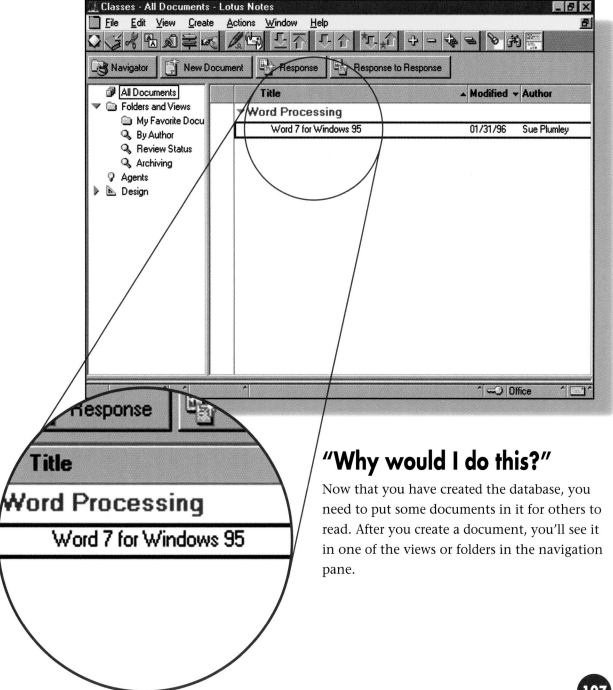

"Why would I do this?"

Now that you have created the database, you need to put some documents in it for others to read. After you create a document, you'll see it in one of the views or folders in the navigation pane.

1 Click the **New Document** button in the action bar. Notes displays a new document ready for you to complete. The square brackets represent the places on the form where you can enter information.

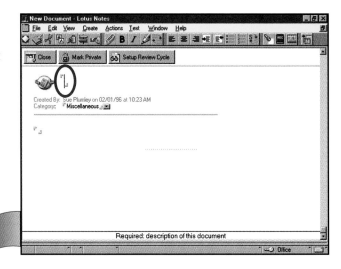

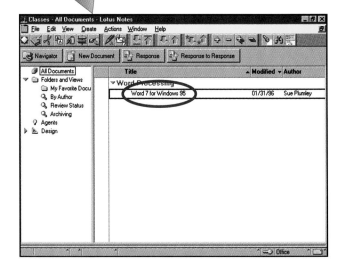

2 At the top of the document, fill in a title for the document as you want it to appear in the view pane; for example, Word 7 for Windows 95. Finish the rest of the form as appropriate, and click the **Close** button in the action bar.

WHY WORRY?

Most of the rest of the tasks in this part teach you techniques to use while creating or editing documents.

3 Notes asks if you want to save the document. Choose **Yes**. Notes redisplays the database, and your document appears in the view pane. ■

Selecting Text

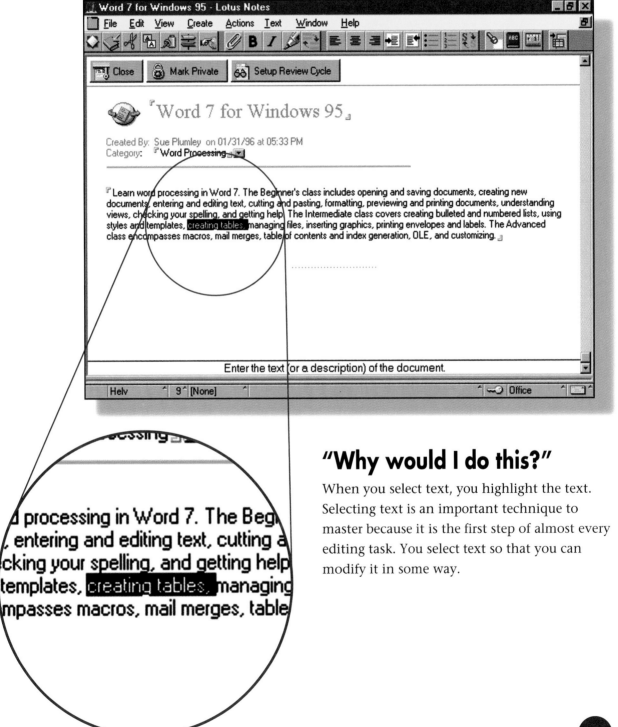

"Why would I do this?"

When you select text, you highlight the text. Selecting text is an important technique to master because it is the first step of almost every editing task. You select text so that you can modify it in some way.

1 To open a document in edit mode, point at the document, press the right mouse button, and choose **Edit** from the shortcut menu.

WHY WORRY?

If you make a mistake, click anywhere in the document to cancel your selection and try again.

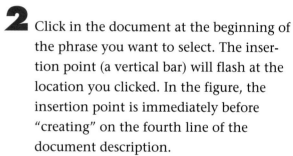

2 Click in the document at the beginning of the phrase you want to select. The insertion point (a vertical bar) will flash at the location you clicked. In the figure, the insertion point is immediately before "creating" on the fourth line of the document description.

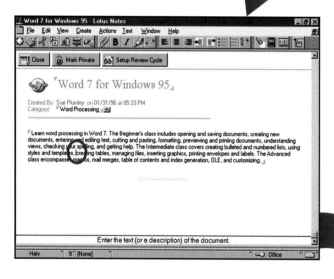

3 Press and hold the left mouse button while you move the mouse to select the text. Selected text appears white against a black background. ■

NOTE ▼

You can use the keyboard to select text. With the insertion point just before the first character you want to select, press and hold the Shift key while pressing the right arrow key until all desired text appears highlighted.

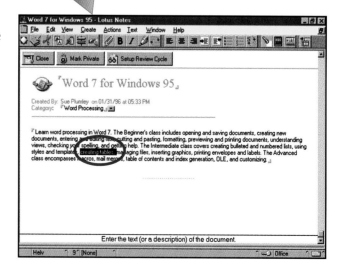

Moving and Copying Text

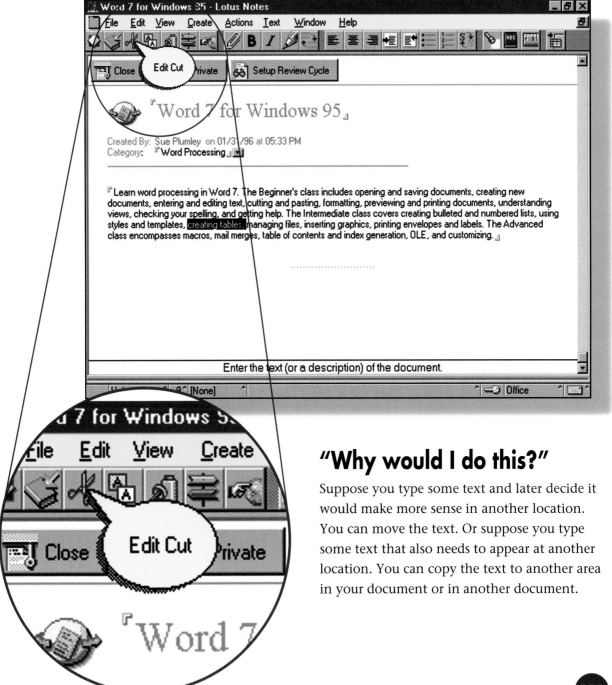

"Why would I do this?"

Suppose you type some text and later decide it would make more sense in another location. You can move the text. Or suppose you type some text that also needs to appear at another location. You can copy the text to another area in your document or in another document.

1 In a document you opened to edit, select the text you want to move or copy.

NOTE ▼

To open a document to edit it, highlight it in the view pane, right-click the mouse, and choose Edit.

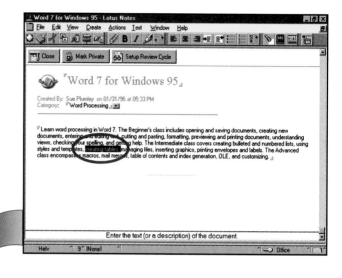

2 To move the text, click the **Cut** SmartIcon. Or open the **Edit** menu and choose the **Cut** command. Notes removes the highlighted text.

NOTE ▼

To copy the text, click the Copy SmartIcon (immediately to the right of the Cut SmartIcon) or open the Edit menu and choose the Copy command.

3 Place the insertion point immediately *after* where you want the text to appear and click the **Paste** SmartIcon. Notes displays the text at the new location in front of the insertion point. ■

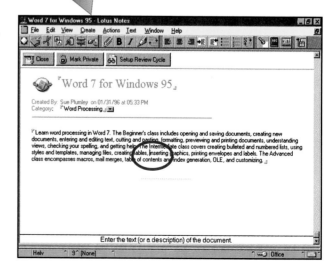

Undoing Changes

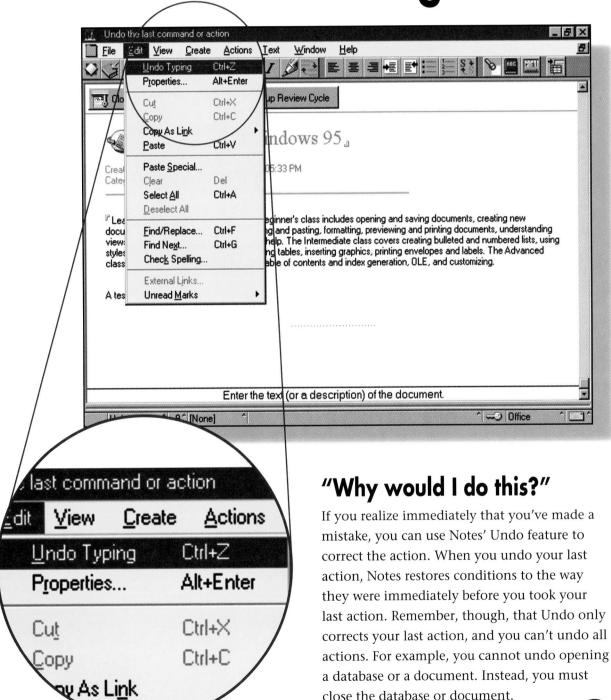

"Why would I do this?"

If you realize immediately that you've made a mistake, you can use Notes' Undo feature to correct the action. When you undo your last action, Notes restores conditions to the way they were immediately before you took your last action. Remember, though, that Undo only corrects your last action, and you can't undo all actions. For example, you cannot undo opening a database or a document. Instead, you must close the database or document.

1 Open a document in edit mode and type some text.

NOTE ▼

To open a document to edit it, highlight it in the view pane, right-click the mouse, and choose Edit.

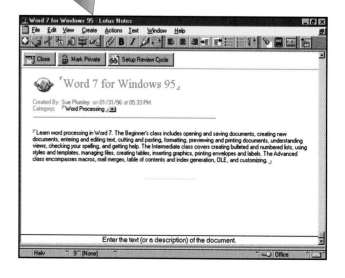

2 Open the **Edit** menu and choose the **Undo Typing** command.

NOTE ▼

You may not always see "Undo Typing" because the word after "Undo" changes, depending on the action you are undoing.

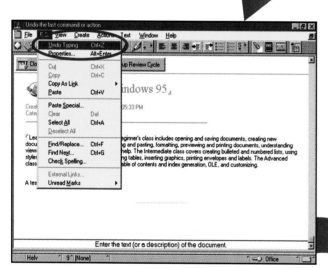

3 Notes removes the typing from your screen. ■

Enhancing Text

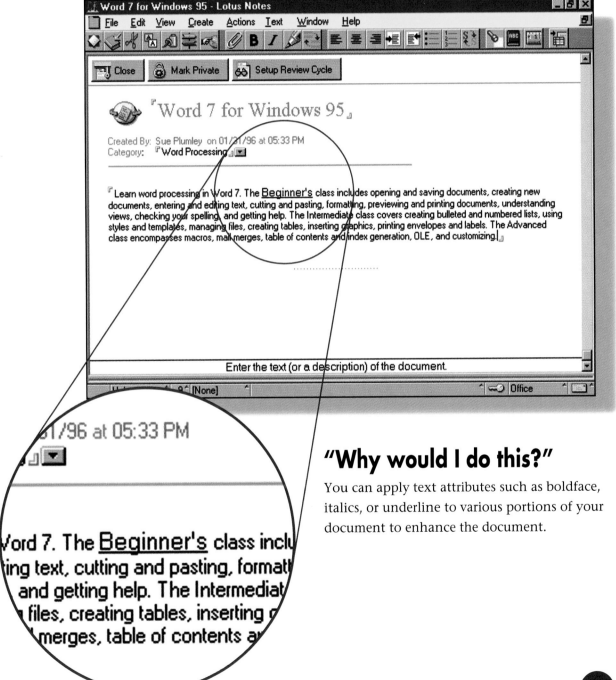

"Why would I do this?"

You can apply text attributes such as boldface, italics, or underline to various portions of your document to enhance the document.

1 In a document opened in edit mode, select the text you want to enhance.

WHY WORRY?

When you apply Bold, Italic, or Underline, you'll see a check mark next to them on the menu. To remove one of these enhancements, reopen the menu and choose the enhancement again. To remove all of them, reopen the Text menu and choose Normal Text.

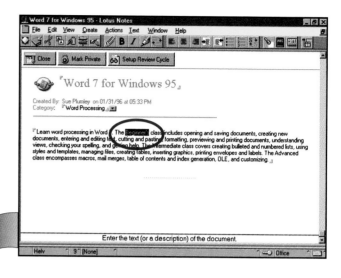

2 Open the Text menu and choose the enhancement you want to make, such as underlining. You can choose from the choices listed in the third section of the menu.

NOTE

If you're applying boldface or italics, you can click the Text Bold or Text Italic SmartIcons.

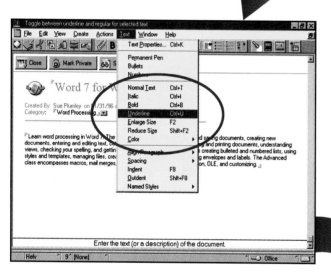

3 To enlarge the selected text, reopen the **Text** menu and choose **Enlarge Size**. Notes makes the selected text bigger. ■

WHY WORRY?

When you choose Reduce Size from the Text menu, Notes reduces the size of selected text in the same increments it increases size.

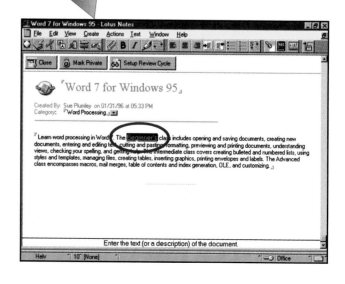

Inserting Page Breaks

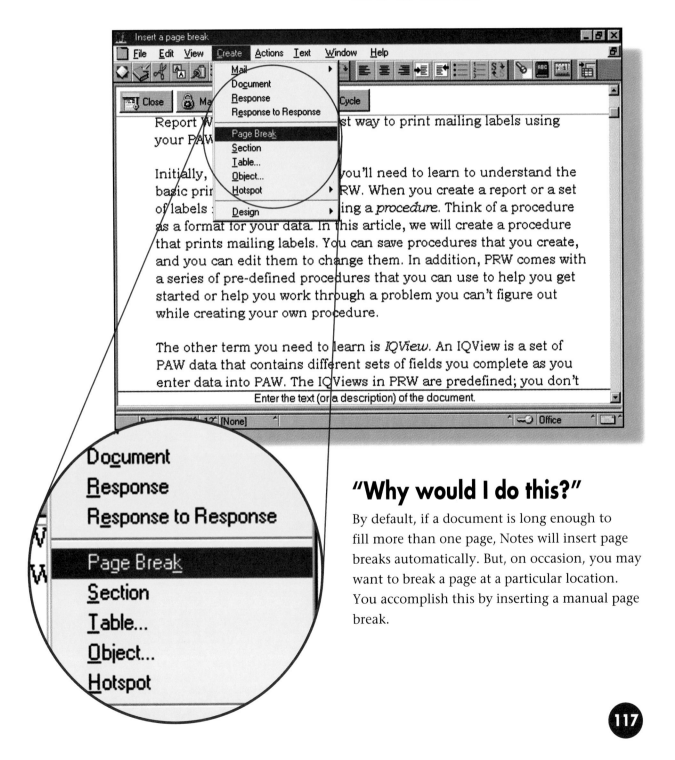

"Why would I do this?"

By default, if a document is long enough to fill more than one page, Notes will insert page breaks automatically. But, on occasion, you may want to break a page at a particular location. You accomplish this by inserting a manual page break.

1 In a document opened in edit mode, place the insertion point anywhere in the paragraph you want to start the new page. In the figure, the insertion point is at the beginning of the paragraph at the bottom of the page.

NOTE ▼

To open a document to edit it, highlight it in the view pane, right-click the mouse, and choose Edit.

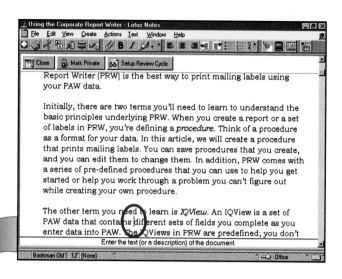

2 Open the **Create** menu and choose **Page Break**.

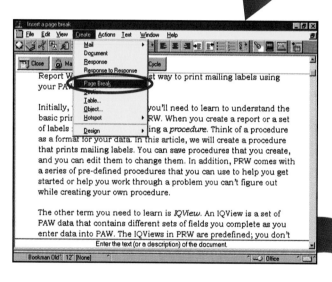

3 Notes displays a solid line immediately above the location of the insertion point. ■

WHY WORRY?

To remove a manual page break, position the insertion point in the paragraph immediately following the page break. Then, reopen the Create menu and choose Page Break again.

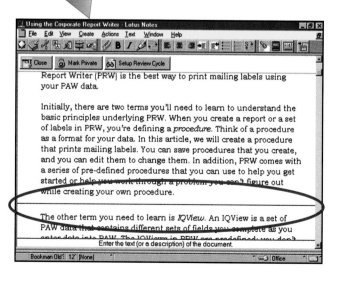

Creating Page Headers and Footers

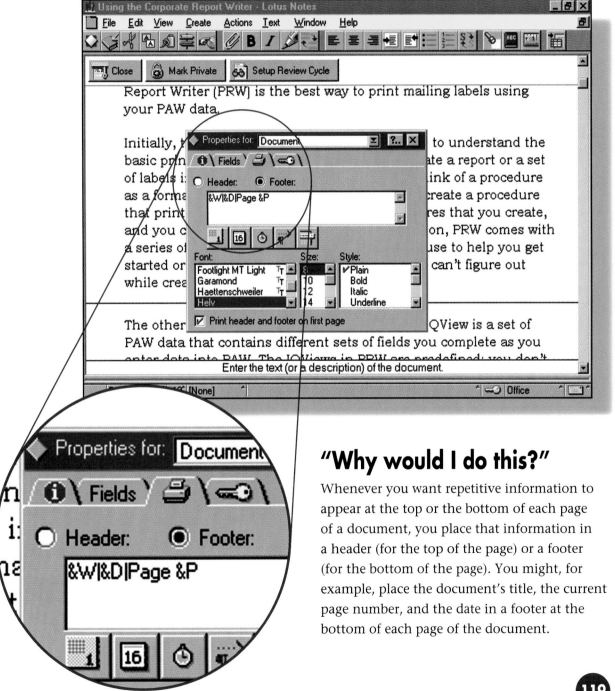

"Why would I do this?"

Whenever you want repetitive information to appear at the top or the bottom of each page of a document, you place that information in a header (for the top of the page) or a footer (for the bottom of the page). You might, for example, place the document's title, the current page number, and the date in a footer at the bottom of each page of the document.

1 In a document opened in edit mode, open the **File** menu and choose **Document Properties**. Notes displays the Document Properties InfoBox.

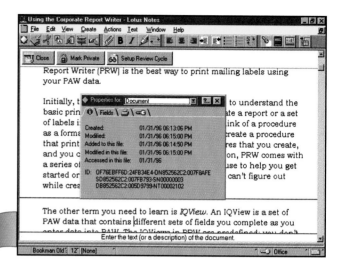

2 Click the printer on the third tab to display that tab.

> **NOTE** ▼
>
> Headers and footers do not appear on-screen; you'll see the header or footer when you print the document.

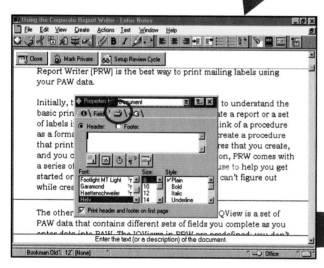

3 Click an option button to choose between a header and a footer.

> **WHY WORRY?**
>
> See the table at the end of this task for information on these buttons.

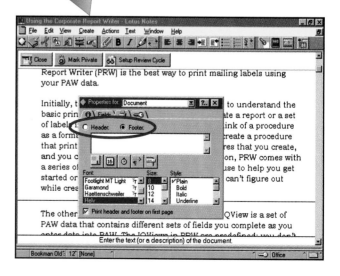

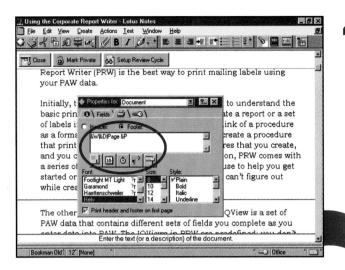

4 In the text box below the option buttons, type the information you want to appear in the header or footer. Use the buttons below the text box to automatically insert document information in the header or footer. In the figure, I added the document's title, a tab, the printing date, another tab, the word "Page," a space, and the current page number inserted. Note that I had to manually type "Page."

5 Optionally, change the header's or footer's font, size, and style, and remove the check mark at the bottom of the box if you don't want the header or footer to print on the first page of the document. Click the **X** in the upper right corner of the box to close the box. ■

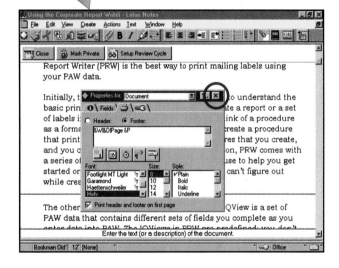

WHY WORRY?

To remove a header or footer, delete the text on the Printer tab of the Document Properties InfoBox.

Inserts the page number.

Inserts the date the document is printed.

Inserts the time the document is printed.

Inserts a tab; use this, for example, to insert a date and a page number on the same line but with space between them.

Inserts the document's title.

TASK 43
Aligning Paragraphs

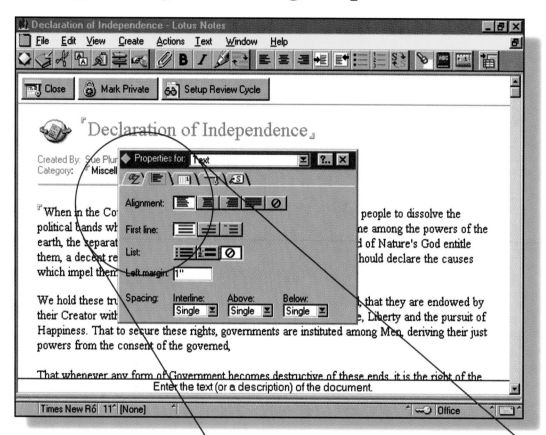

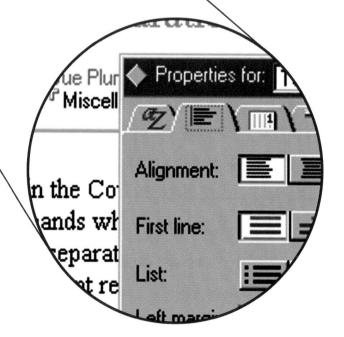

"Why would I do this?"

You may have occasion to align the paragraphs of your document other than the standard default alignment, which is on the left margin. You can, in a Notes document, align a paragraph on the left margin, on the right margin, centered between the left and right margins, aligned on both the left and right margins so that no ragged edges appear, or all on one line, without word wrap operating.

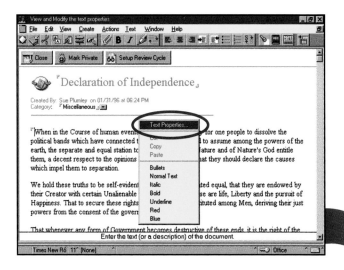

1 In a document opened in edit mode, place the insertion point in the paragraph you want to realign, and press the right mouse button to display a shortcut menu. Choose **Text Properties**.

2 Notes displays the Text Properties InfoBox.

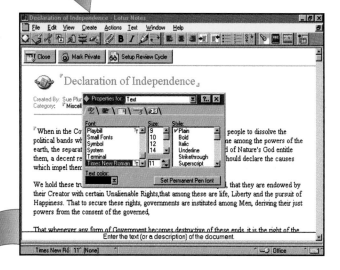

3 Click the second tab, the **Alignment** tab.

4 Use one of the alignment buttons to choose an alignment for the current paragraph. This figure shows the first paragraph aligned at the left margin.

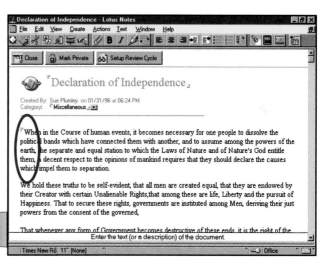

5 This figure shows the first paragraph centered between the left and right margins.

6 In this figure, the first paragraph is aligned on the right margin.

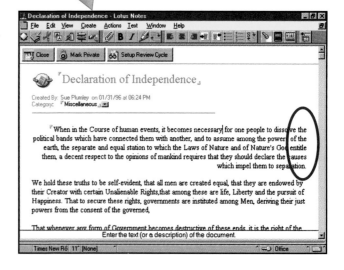

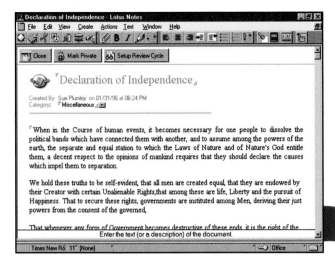

7 In this paragraph, the first paragraph is aligned to both margins. Notice that the paragraph has no ragged edges.

8 This figure shows only part of the first paragraph because the paragraph has no alignment and word wrap isn't operating. ∎

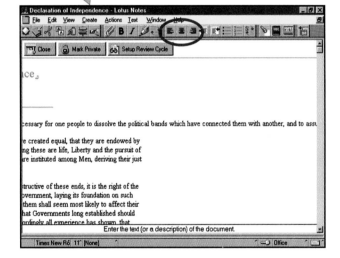

> **NOTE** ▼
>
> As a shortcut, use the Align Left, Align Center, and Align Right SmartIcons.

Indenting Paragraphs

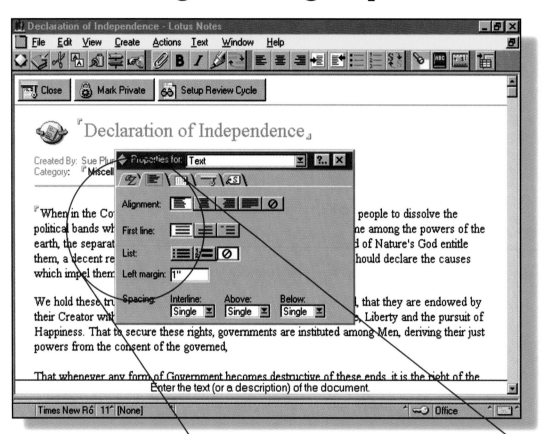

"Why would I do this?"

Sometimes, you need to indent paragraphs for emphasis. In Notes, you can indent the entire paragraph, just the first line of the paragraph, or all lines of the paragraph *except* the first line.

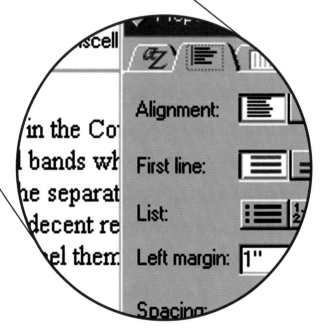

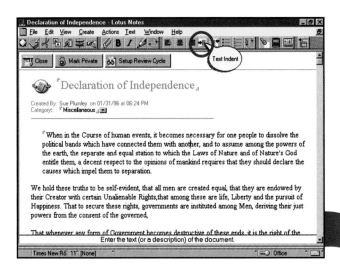

1 In a document opened in edit mode, place the insertion point in the paragraph you want to indent. To indent the entire paragraph, click the **Indent** SmartIcon. Each time you click the Indent SmartIcon, Notes indents the current paragraph 1/4 inch.

WHY WORRY?

To move the paragraph back toward the left margin (or "outdent"), click the Outdent SmartIcon, immediately to the right of the Indent SmartIcon.

2 To indent just the first line of a paragraph or all lines except the first, use the Text Properties InfoBox. Right click over a paragraph and choose **Text Properties**.

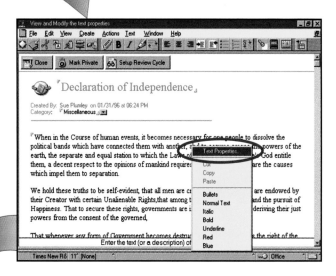

3 After the InfoBox appears, click the second tab. Note the three buttons labeled First Line.

4 Click the middle button to indent the first line of the paragraph.

NOTE ▼

Double-click the title bar of the Text Properties InfoBox to reduce its size so that you can see the results of your choice. Double-click the title bar again to restore its size.

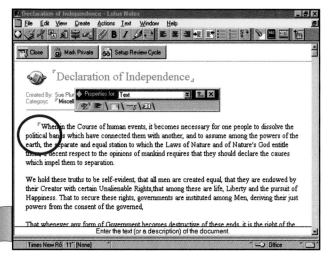

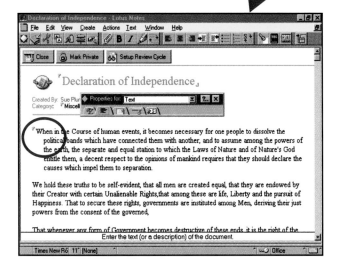

5 Click the right button to indent all lines of the paragraph *except* the first line. ■

Listing Items Using Bullets or Numbers

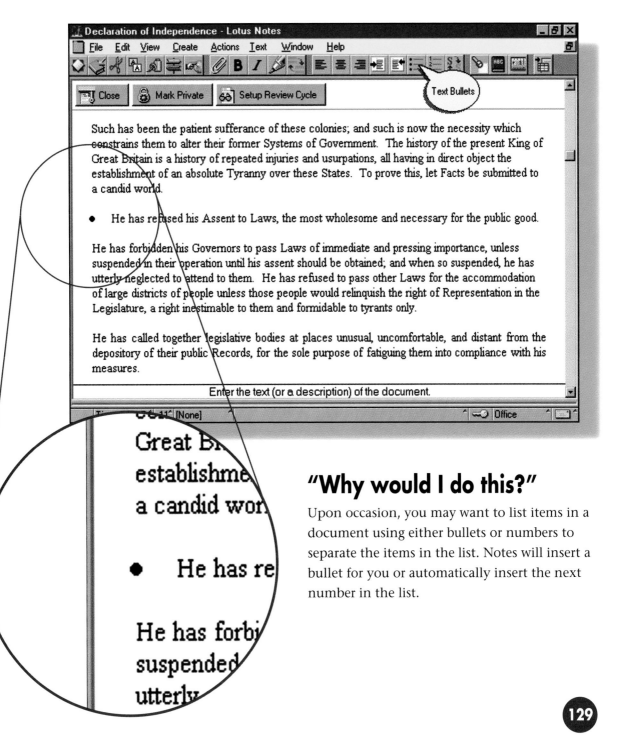

"Why would I do this?"

Upon occasion, you may want to list items in a document using either bullets or numbers to separate the items in the list. Notes will insert a bullet for you or automatically insert the next number in the list.

1 In a document opened in edit mode, place the insertion point in the paragraph to which you want to add a bullet or number.

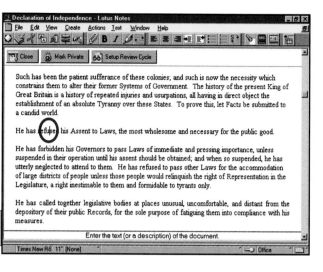

2 To add a bullet before the paragraph, click the **Text Bullets** SmartIcon.

WHY WORRY?

To remove a bullet, place the insertion point anywhere in a paragraph containing a bullet and click the Text Bullets SmartIcon.

3 To add a number to the paragraph containing the insertion point, click the **Text Numbers** SmartIcon. ■

WHY WORRY?

You remove a number the same way you remove a bullet; place the insertion point anywhere in the paragraph containing the number and click the Text Numbers SmartIcon.

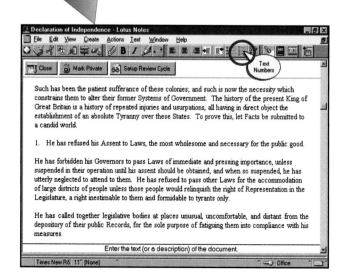

Setting Tabs

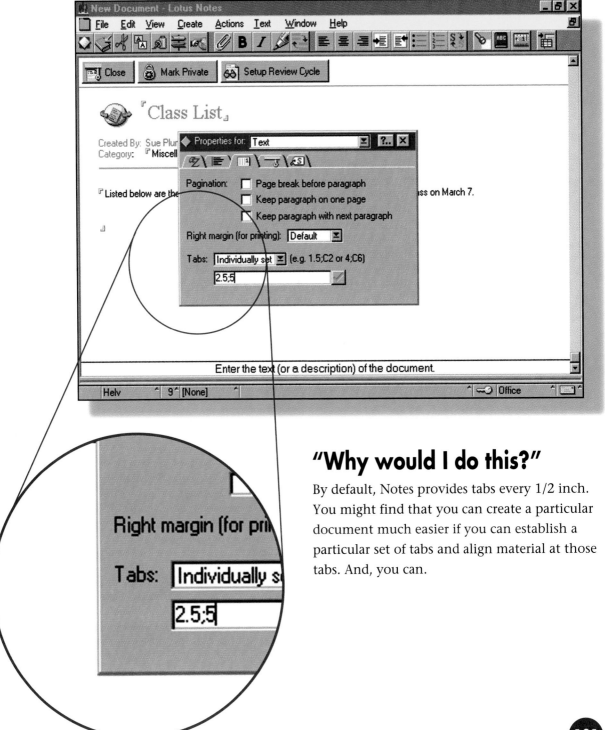

"Why would I do this?"

By default, Notes provides tabs every 1/2 inch. You might find that you can create a particular document much easier if you can establish a particular set of tabs and align material at those tabs. And, you can.

1 In a document opened in edit mode, place the insertion point at the location where you want the tab settings to take effect. Click the right mouse button to display a shortcut menu. Choose **Text Properties**.

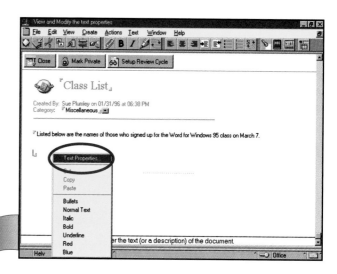

2 When the Text Properties InfoBox appears, click the third tab.

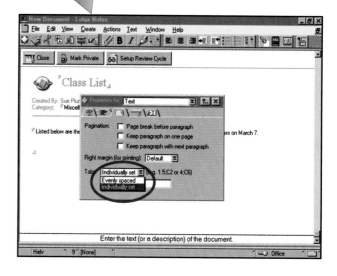

3 To set tabs that are equal distances apart, choose **Evenly spaced** from the Tabs list box. To set tabs at specific locations, choose **Individually set** from the Tabs list box.

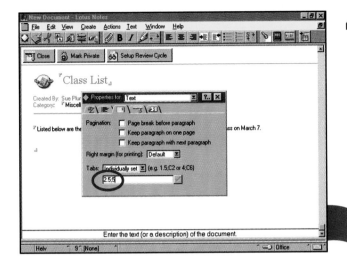

4 In the text box below the Tab list box, type the location, in inches, where you want Notes to set tabs.

NOTE ▼

To set more than one tab, separate the numbers by a semicolon (;).

5 Close the Text Properties InfoBox (click the **X** in the upper right corner of the box), and type in your document. You'll find tabs at the locations you specified. ■

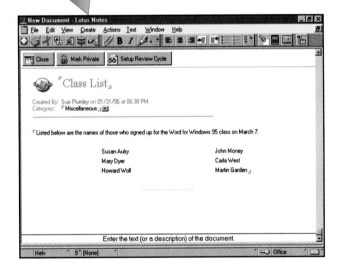

Creating Tables

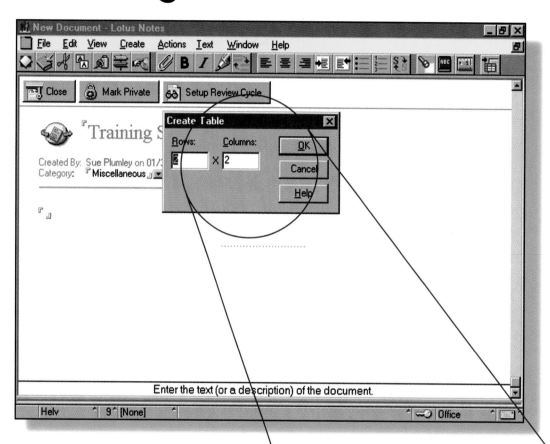

"Why would I do this?"

Sometimes, tables work more efficiently than setting tabs, particularly when you need to organize your information into multiple columns. You can create tables in a Notes document.

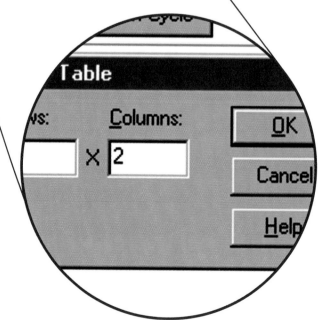

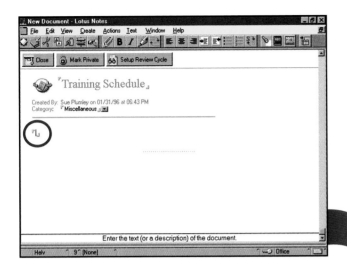

1 Open a new document or open an existing document in edit mode and place the insertion point where you want the table to appear.

2 Open the **Create** menu and choose **Table**. Notes displays the Create Table dialog box.

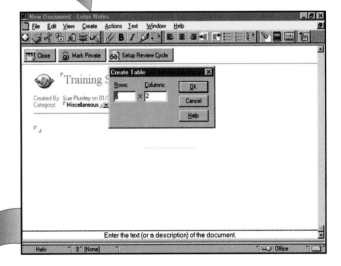

3 Type the number of rows and columns you want for your table and choose **OK**. Notes displays the table in your document. ■

WHY WORRY?

Use the commands on the Table menu to format your table.

Finding and Replacing Text

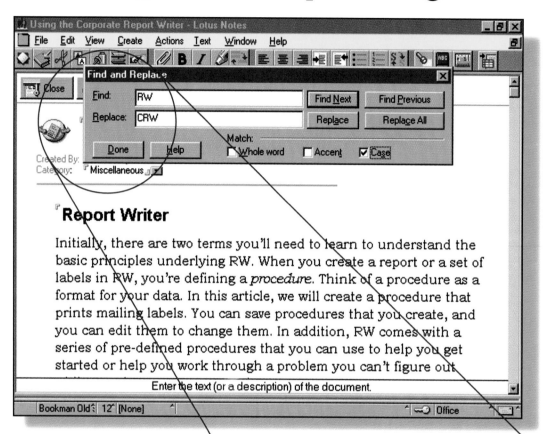

"Why would I do this?"

Suppose you create a rather lengthy document. When you finish and reread the document, you decide that you want to change a particular phrase you used throughout the document. You can use the Find and Replace feature in Notes to find text in documents and change it.

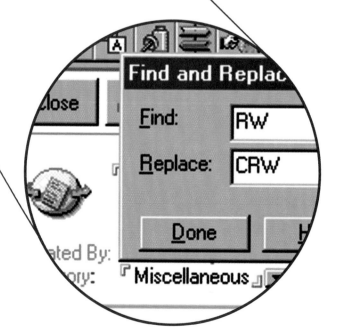

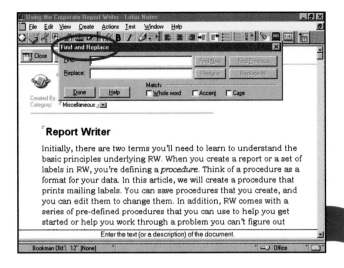

1 Open an existing document in edit mode and place the insertion point at the top of the document. Then, open the **Edit** menu and choose the **Find/Replace** command.

2 In the Find text box, type the word or words for which you want Notes to search.

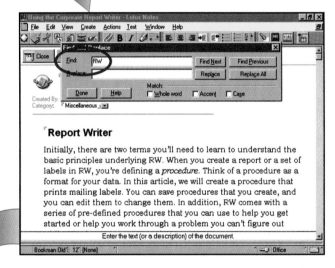

3 In the Replace text box, type the word or words you want Notes to substitute each time it finds the word for which you are searching.

4 Use the check boxes at the bottom of the Find and Replace dialog box to specify your search more exactly. For example, place a check in the **Case** check box if you want Notes to search for words that match the capitalization you used in the Find text box.

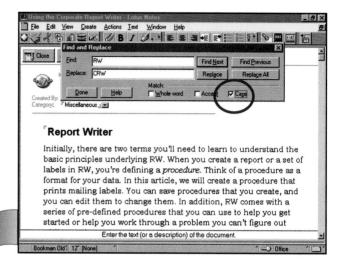

5 Choose **Find Next** to find the next occurrence of the text for which you're searching.

NOTE ▼

To change *all* occurrences of the text you typed in the Find box, choose Replace All. If you choose Replace All, Notes warns you that you cannot undo the results of Replace All and gives you the opportunity to cancel the operation.

6 Choose **Replace** to replace the occurrence Notes found with the text you typed in the Replace box. When you finish searching and replacing, choose **Done** to close the Find and Replace text box. ■

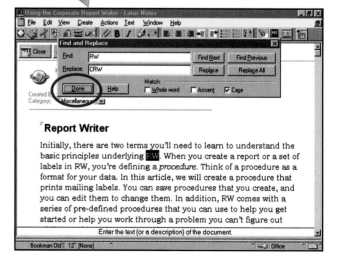

Checking Spelling

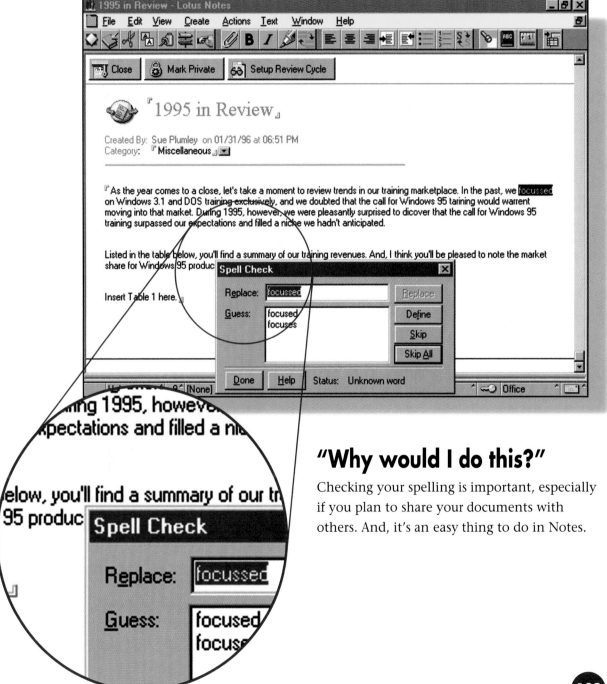

"Why would I do this?"

Checking your spelling is important, especially if you plan to share your documents with others. And, it's an easy thing to do in Notes.

1 Open an existing document in edit mode and place the insertion point at the top of the document.

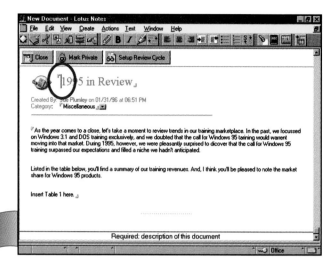

2 Open the **Edit** menu and choose the **Check Spelling** command. Notes highlights the first misspelled word it finds in your document and attempts to suggest the correct spelling.

3 Choose a word from the Guess list box and then choose **Replace**.

NOTE ▼

If the word is one you use commonly but isn't in the Notes dictionary (such as an acronym of your company's name), choose Define to add it to the dictionary.

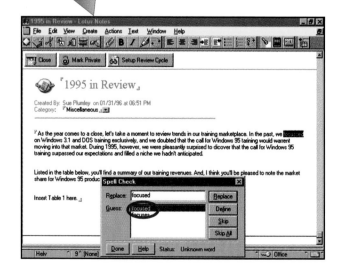

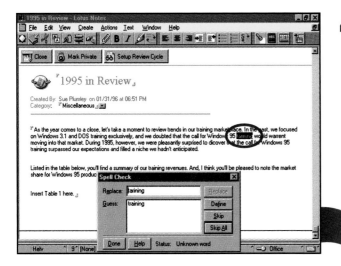

4 Notes continues checking and identifies the next incorrectly spelled word. Again, choose a word from the Guess list box or choose either **Define** or **Skip**.

WHY WORRY?

If the word is spelled correctly but you don't use it often enough to add it to the Notes dictionary, choose Skip.

5 After Notes finishes checking your document, you'll see the dialog box in this figure. ■

WHY WORRY?

Don't forget to save your document to save the changes made during Spell checking.

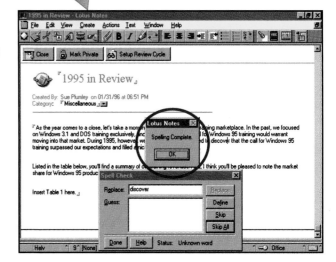

TASK 50

Working with DocLinks

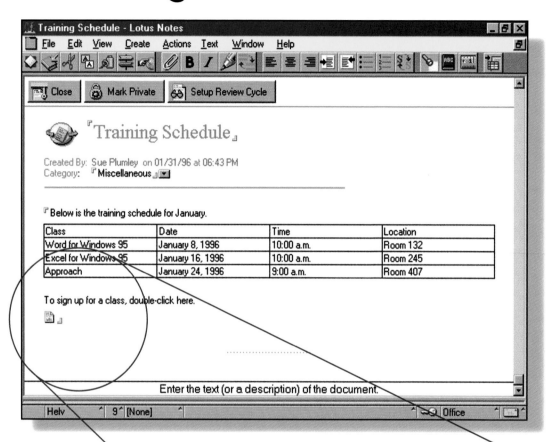

"Why would I do this?"

A *DocLink* is an icon you see in database documents that switches a user from the current document to a different document, view, folder, or database in Notes. A DocLink differs from an attachment (you learned about attachments in Part II) because an attachment switches a reader to a file created outside Notes. When you use a DocLink, you stay in Notes. Suppose you want to create a link in your database that switches a user from the current document to a different document, view, folder, or database in Notes.

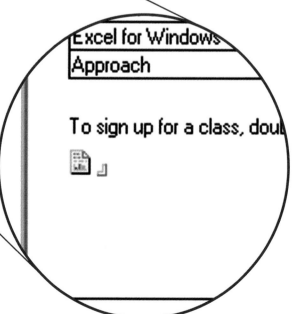

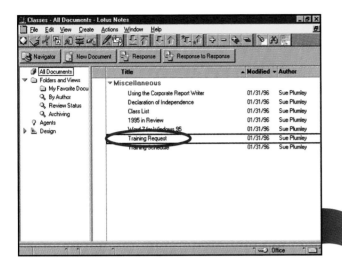

1 In the View pane, select the document you want to display when a user activates a DocLink.

NOTE ▼

You can create a DocLink to a view or folder or to another database. In the Navigation pane, select the view or folder you want to display. From a workspace tab, select the database you want to display.

2 Click the right mouse button and choose the **Copy As Link** command from the shortcut menu. The hourglass icon appears while Notes stores the information. After the hourglass disappears, look at the center status bar at the bottom of the screen to see a message telling you that a DocLink was copied to the Clipboard.

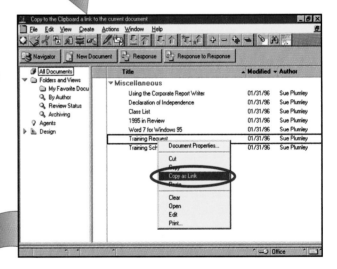

3 Open, in edit mode, the document readers will be reading when they use the DocLink. Place the insertion point at the spot where the link should appear, type some text, and click the **Paste** SmartIcon. Notes displays a DocLink in the open document.

4 To test the DocLink, make sure you're viewing the document that contains the DocLink. You don't need to be in edit mode. Double-click the DocLink.

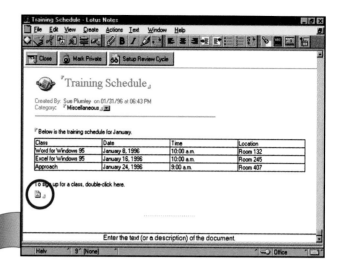

5 Notes switches to the element attached to the DocLink. To return to the original document, press **Esc**. ■

Inserting a
Pop-Up Hotspot

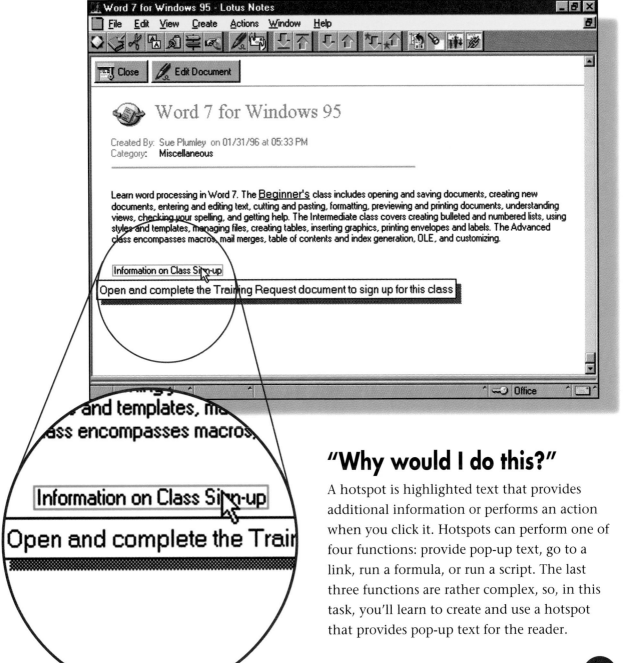

"Why would I do this?"

A hotspot is highlighted text that provides additional information or performs an action when you click it. Hotspots can perform one of four functions: provide pop-up text, go to a link, run a formula, or run a script. The last three functions are rather complex, so, in this task, you'll learn to create and use a hotspot that provides pop-up text for the reader.

1 Open, in edit mode, the document to which you want to add a hotspot.

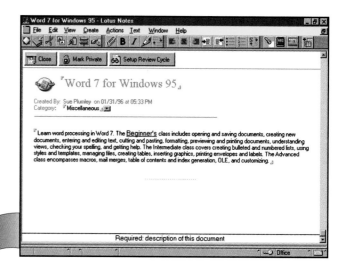

2 Type and select the text you want the reader to see that lets him know this is a pop-up. The selected text will become the pop-up.

3 Open the **Create** menu and **choose Hotspot**. From the submenu, choose **Text Popup**. Notes displays the HotSpot Popup Properties InfoBox.

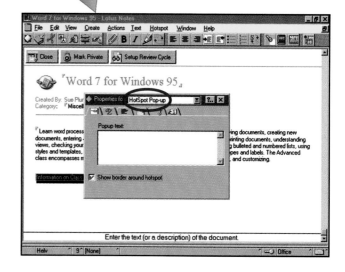

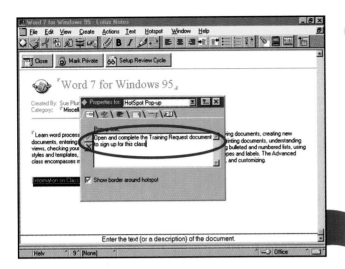

4 In the Popup text list box, type the text you want to appear when the reader clicks on the hotspot. Click the check mark to the left of the box when you finish to save the text.

5 To test the hotspot, close the InfoBox, save and close the document, and reopen it— but not in edit mode. Click and hold the mouse button over the hotspot. ■

NOTE ▼

You can enhance the hotspot using the tabs in the HotSpot Properties InfoBox. Put the document in edit mode and right-click the hotspot to display a shortcut menu, from which you can choose HotSpot Properties to open the InfoBox.

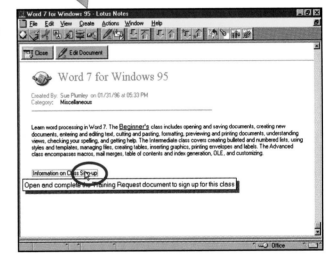

Importing Data

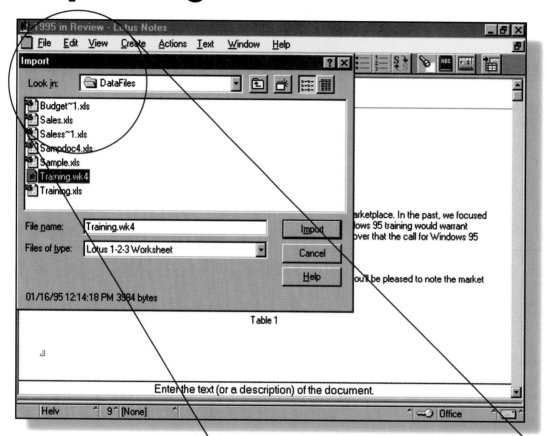

"Why would I do this?"

There are times when you'd feel more comfortable creating a document in another program, but you need the information from that document in a Notes document. You can create and save a file in another program and then import the information into a Notes document. That way, you can work in the program where you are most comfortable but still save time by not re-creating the information in Notes.

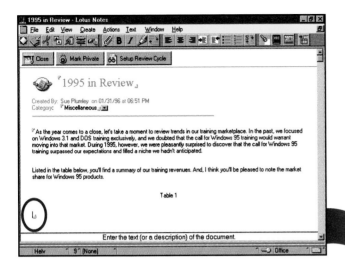

1 Open, in edit mode, the document into which you want to import information and place the insertion point at the location where you want the information to appear.

2 Open the **File** menu and choose the **Import** command. Notes displays the Import dialog box, from which you choose a document to import.

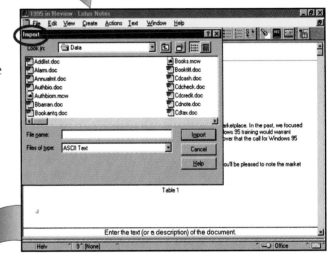

3 Navigate to the folder containing the file you want to import; highlight the file.

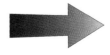

4 If Notes doesn't display the correct file type, open the **Files of type** list box and choose the type of file you intend to import. Then, choose the **Import** button.

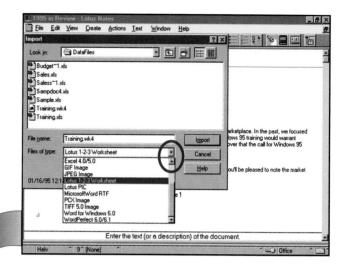

5 The contents of the imported file appear in your Notes document. ■

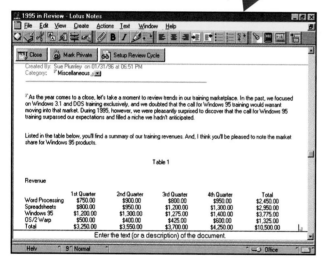

Creating Categories

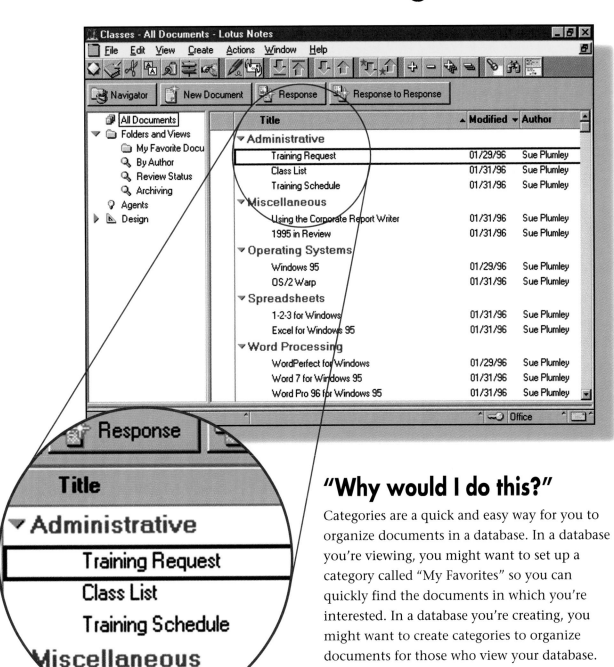

"Why would I do this?"

Categories are a quick and easy way for you to organize documents in a database. In a database you're viewing, you might want to set up a category called "My Favorites" so you can quickly find the documents in which you're interested. In a database you're creating, you might want to create categories to organize documents for those who view your database.

1 Open, in edit mode, the first document you want to place in a category. Click the down arrow next to the category field. The field currently contains the word Miscellaneous.

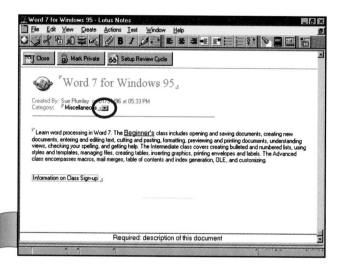

2 Notes displays the Select Keywords dialog box. Click **Miscellaneous** in the list to deselect it.

3 In the New Keywords text box at the bottom of the dialog box, type the name you want to use as the category for the open document.

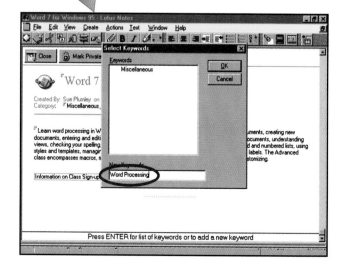

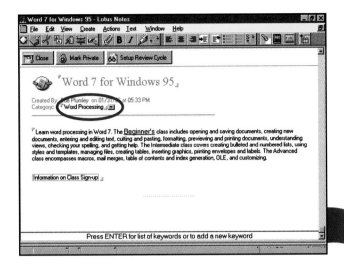

4 When you choose **OK,** Notes changes the category of the document to the new category you created.

5 Save and close the document. Then, repeat these steps until you have categorized all the documents you want to categorize. ∎

WHY WORRY?

Once you create a category, you'll see it in the list. You can select it by clicking and deselect any other categories by clicking them to remove the check mark. Or you can assign more than one category to a document by leaving multiple keywords selected.

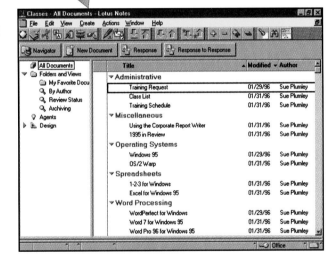

Looking at Documents in Different Ways

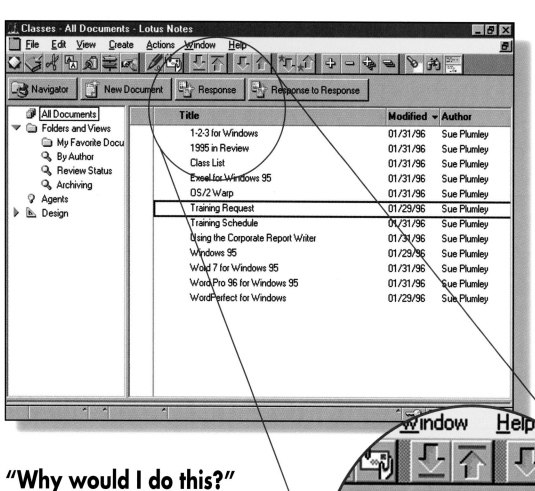

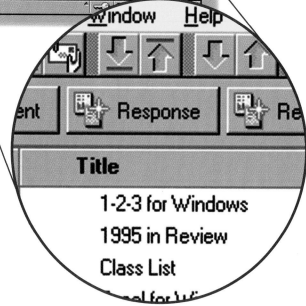

"Why would I do this?"

Once you categorize documents, you can view the documents by category, or you can tell Notes to ignore the categories and display the documents in alphabetical order by name. You also can organize documents by date—either earliest to latest or latest to earliest. And, you can do all this from within one view of the database.

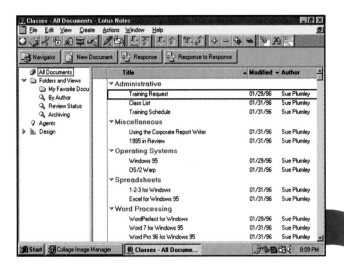

1 Open the database containing the categories you set up and display the View pane. In the figure, you see the documents organized by category; and the categories are in alphabetical order.

2 To hide the categories and display the documents in alphabetical order, click anywhere in the gray bar where the word **Title** appears.

The caret next to the word "Title" changes colors when you click the bar.

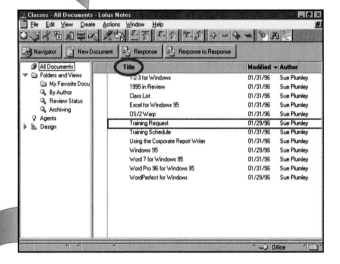

3 To display the documents based on creation date, click the portion of the gray bar where the word Modified appears. Notes changes the order of the documents so that you view them from newest to oldest. ■

WHY WORRY?

To redisplay documents by categories, click the bar again.

Placing Your Database on the Server

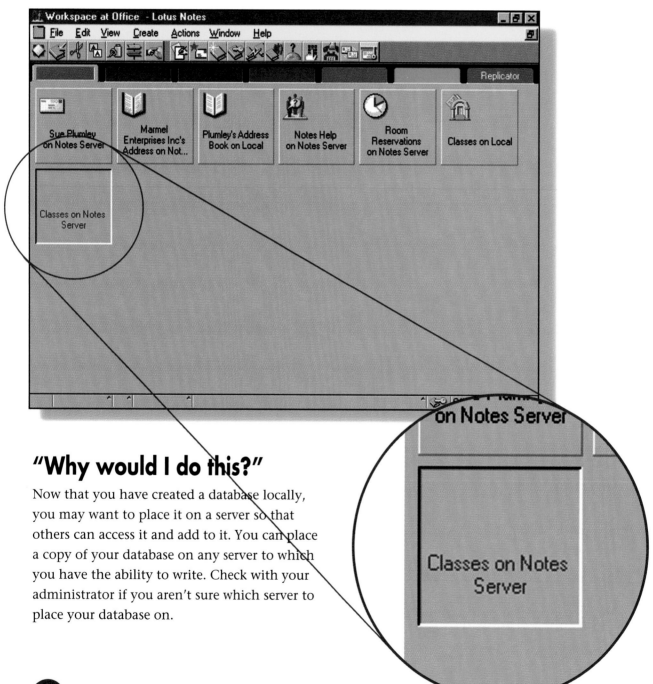

"Why would I do this?"

Now that you have created a database locally, you may want to place it on a server so that others can access it and add to it. You can place a copy of your database on any server to which you have the ability to write. Check with your administrator if you aren't sure which server to place your database on.

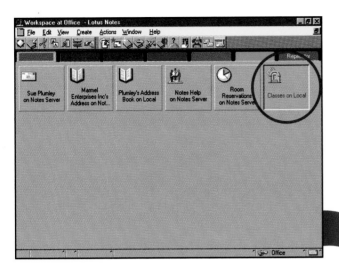

1 Display the workspace tab containing the database you want to place on the Server and select that database.

2 Open the **File** menu and choose **Database**. From the submenu, choose **New Copy**. Notes displays the Copy Database dialog box, and the database you selected in Step 1 appears in the dialog box.

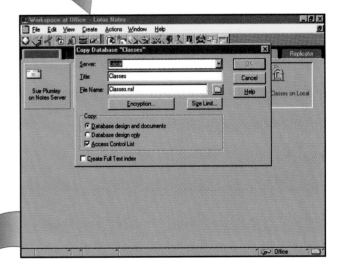

3 Open the **Server** list box and select a server to which to copy the database.

4 Place a check in the **Create Full Text index** check box.

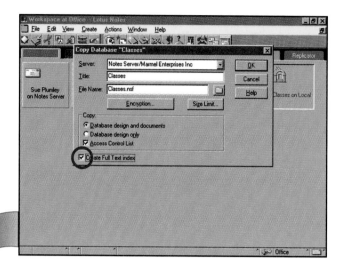

5 Choose **OK**. Notes copies your database to the server you chose. You'll see the dialog box in the figure, which explains that your request to index your database has been queued on the server and you can search the database as soon as Notes finishes indexing.

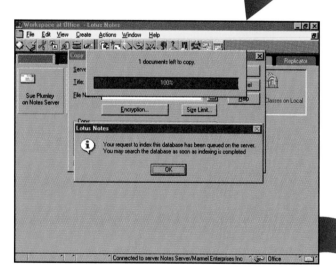

NOTE ▼

You may need to use your password to access the server.

6 Choose **OK**. Notes redisplays your workspace, and you'll see an icon for your database on the server you selected. ■

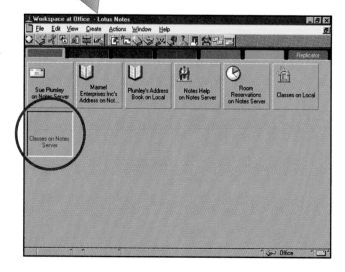

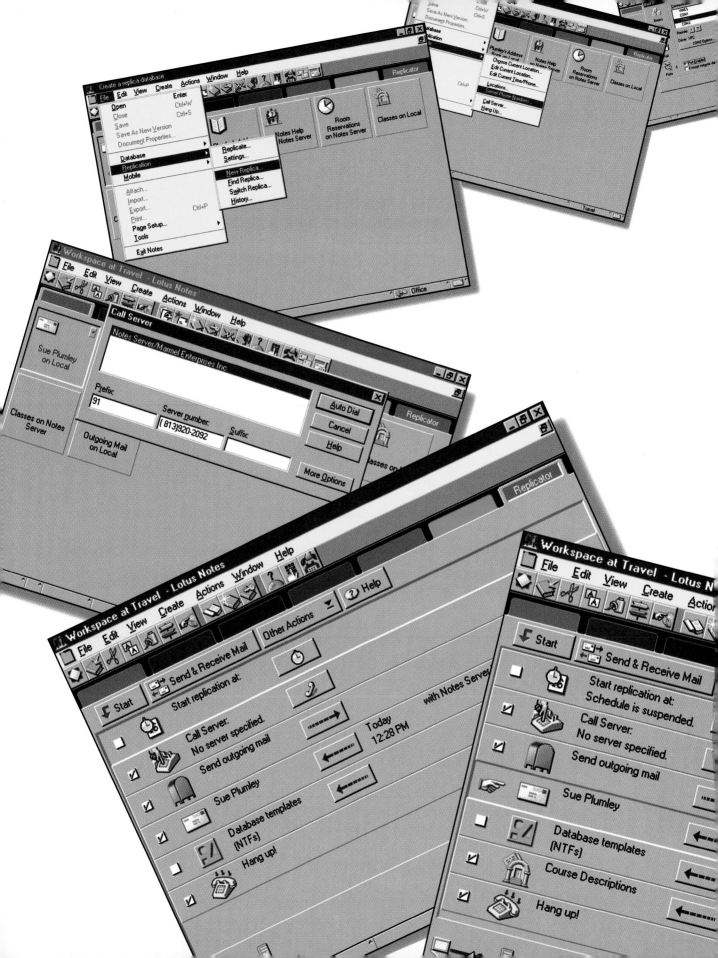

PART V

Notes and Traveling

Until now, we've virtually ignored the fact that you can use Notes not only from the computer on your desk, but also from the computer you travel with—or even the computer you have at home. The computer you use is referred to as the Notes Client machine; you connect that machine to the Notes Server, which manages all the activities you do while working in Notes. The Notes Server puts your mail in your mailbox, and the databases you access and create are stored on the Notes Server. While you work in the office, you typically connect to the Notes Server through your company's network. When you're away from the office, you typically connect to the Notes Server using a *modem*, a piece of hardware inserted in your computer that works with a telephone. With the modem in your computer, you create a "dial-up" connection to the Notes Server.

It's important to understand that you can do the same work in Notes whether you use a dial-up connection or whether you connect in your office over the network. The only difference is how you "connect." In this part, the first three tasks teach you how to set things up before you go on the road. If you use a notebook computer while you're away from the office, you should test your connection before you actually go on the road; just complete the first three tasks in this part and then use a phone line in your office to dial into the Notes Server. That way, you'll know that "everything works" before you leave town.

If you want to work on a database while you're away from the office, you should make a copy of all or part of that database before you go on the road. That way, you can work "offline," without connecting to the Notes Server. By working offline, you can make changes and create documents without running up a phone bill. When you make this type of local copy of a database, the local copy is called a *local replica*.

By the way, you don't have to be "going on the road" to work with a local replica. In Part III, you learned how to make changes to a database while accessing it on the Server. But, you also can make a local replica so that you can make changes to the database while working offline. Working offline on a replica while still at your office has advantages, too. For example, you can work on a database even if the Notes Server is not available.

In Part III, you learned to make a local copy of a database. You may be wondering about the difference between a local copy and a local replica. You create a local copy of a database when you intend to use it exclusively on your computer, and you *don't* intend to send changes to the database back to the server. You might recall the example used in Part III of a company forms database. In this example, we suggested that you might want to copy the forms database to your machine to use, but you wouldn't make changes to the forms and send them back to the server. You'd just use them at your machine. When you want to share changes to a database by sending them back to a server, you use a replica. And, for those of you who care about how Notes knows the difference between a copy and a replica, Notes assigns IDs to each database you create. When you create a new local copy, Notes assigns a unique ID, but when you create a replica, Notes assigns to the replica the same ID the database has on the server.

When you finish working offline, you connect to the Notes Server and send the changes in your local replica to the database on the Notes Server. You use a process called *replication* to send the changes. When Notes replicates, it figures out what changes you have made and incorporates that information into the database on the server without making changes to any other information in the database. Replication is a two-way process; the Notes Server receives the changes you made and, if you want, will send you new changes made by others since the last time you replicated. In the last three tasks in this part, you learn how to connect to the Notes Server using your modem and exchange information with the server.

Setting Up Your Modem for Travel

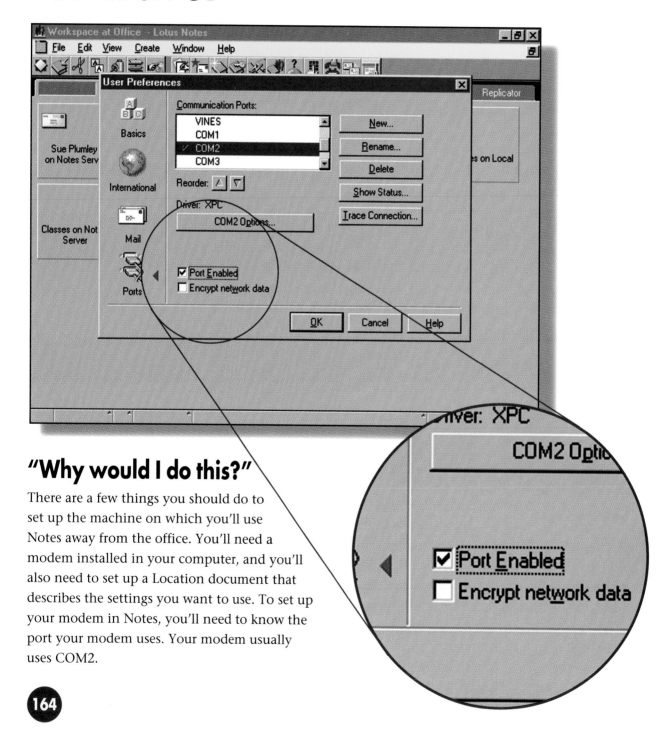

"Why would I do this?"

There are a few things you should do to set up the machine on which you'll use Notes away from the office. You'll need a modem installed in your computer, and you'll also need to set up a Location document that describes the settings you want to use. To set up your modem in Notes, you'll need to know the port your modem uses. Your modem usually uses COM2.

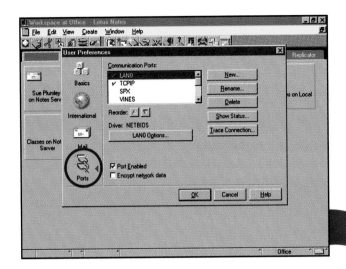

1 Open the **File** menu and choose **Tools**. From the submenu, choose **User Preferences**. In the left side of the User Preferences dialog box, choose **Ports**.

2 In the Communication Ports list, make sure a check mark appears next to the port on which your modem is installed. If you don't see a check mark, highlight the port and choose the **Port Enabled** check box to place a check in it.

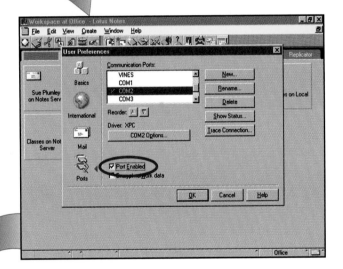

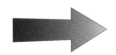

3 (Optional) If you need to select a modem or want to hear the phone dialing when you call into the server, highlight your modem port (for example, COM2). Click the **Options** button for your modem port.

4 To select a modem, open the Modem type list box and choose your modem. If your modem is 100% Hayes-compatible and doesn't appear in the list, use the default of **Auto Configure** and let Notes set up your modem. If your modem is not 100% Hayes-compatible, see your Notes Administrator for help setting up your modem.

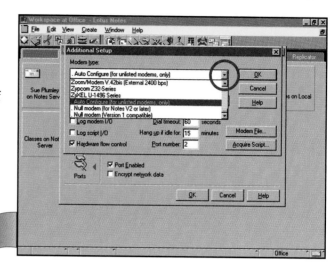

5 In the Additional Setup dialog box, change the Speaker Volume to Low, Medium, or High (Low is usually sufficient). Choose **OK** to close the Additional Setup dialog box and redisplay the User Preferences dialog box.

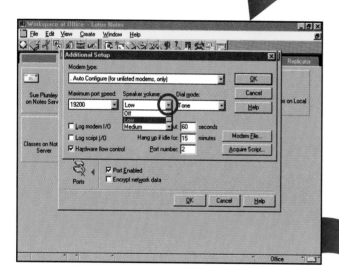

6 Choose **OK** to close the User Preferences dialog box.

WHY WORRY?

If you're working from home, choose Home (Modem).

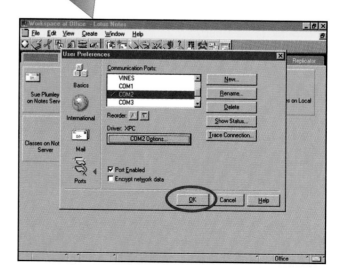

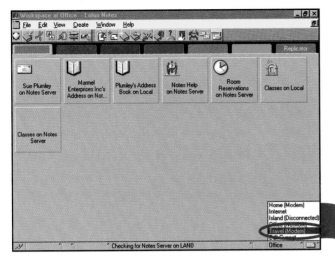

7 In the lower right portion of the status bar, click the box that currently displays **Office**. Notes displays a pop-up menu. Choose **Travel (Modem)**.

The location you select in this pop-up box determines the method you'll use to connect to the Notes Server. Each location corresponds to a location document that describes the settings you want to use to connect to the Notes Server.

8 Notes displays the Time and Phone Information for Travel dialog box. Use this dialog box to enter phone, date, and time information before making a call.

You may want to check your Travel location document to make sure it is correct. Choose **Cancel** to close the Time and Phone Information for Travel dialog box. Then, open the **File** menu and choose **Mobile**. From the sub-menu, choose **Edit Current Location** to view and edit the location document.

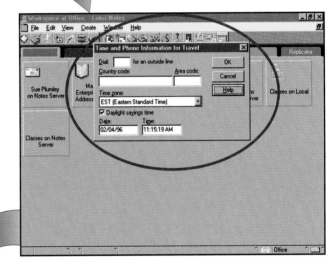

9 Notes adds a new database icon to the workspace and then displays your Travel location document. Your Travel location document should look similar to the one in the figure. Make sure that the port your modem uses is checked and that your server and domain name appear in the Home/mail server field. If you make any changes, save them when you close the document. ∎

Setting Up the Server Phone Number

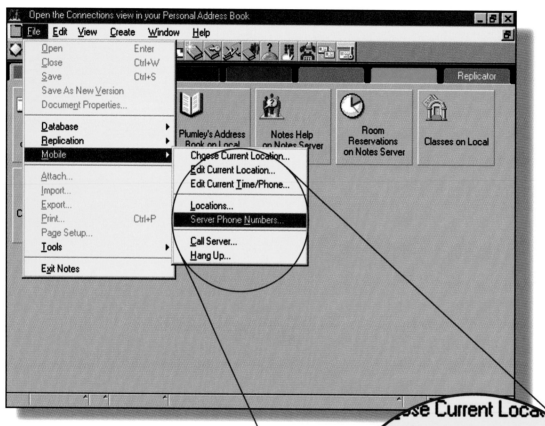

"Why would I do this?"

To use a modem to connect to the Notes Server, your computer uses telephone lines to phone the Notes Server computer. To call your Notes Server, you'll need to tell your computer the phone number to call by creating a Server Connection document.

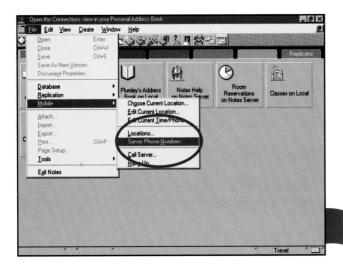

1 Open the **File** menu and choose **Mobile**. From the submenu, choose **Server Phone Numbers**.

2 Click the **Add Connection** button to open a Connection document.

WHY WORRY?

If you don't know your Notes server information, see your Notes Administrator.

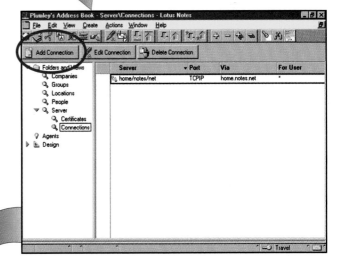

3 Fill in the document so that it resembles the one you see in the figure—using your own Server name, Country code, Area code, and Phone number. Click the arrow next to Advanced to open the bottom portion of the document and change the usage priority to **Normal**. Save the document and close it. ■

Taking a Database on the Road

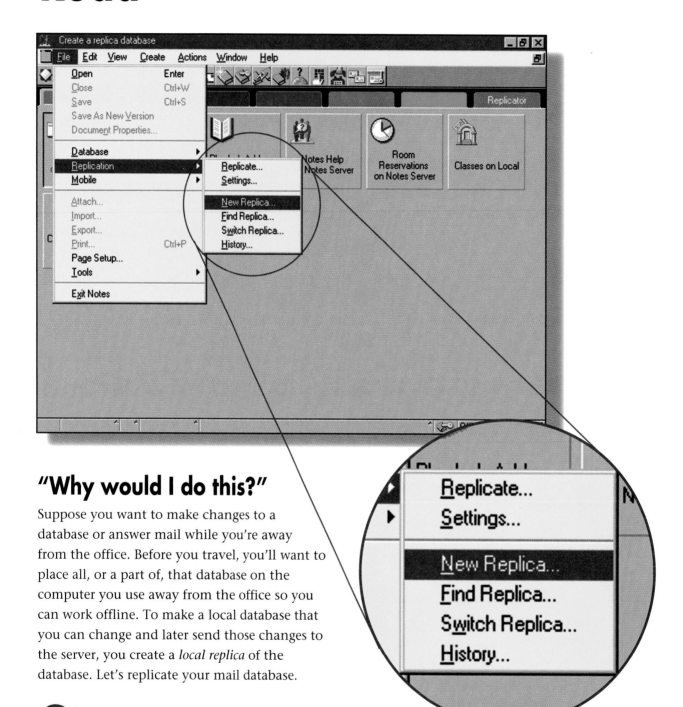

"Why would I do this?"

Suppose you want to make changes to a database or answer mail while you're away from the office. Before you travel, you'll want to place all, or a part of, that database on the computer you use away from the office so you can work offline. To make a local database that you can change and later send those changes to the server, you create a *local replica* of the database. Let's replicate your mail database.

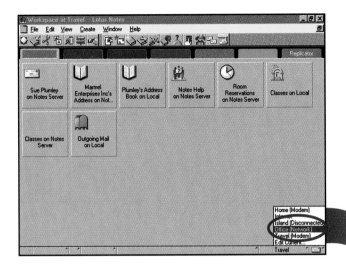

1 (Optional) If you see Travel (Modem) in the box on the lower right portion of the status bar, click the box. Choose **Office (Network)** to connect to your Notes Server through your company network.

NOTE ▼

If your notebook computer doesn't contain a network card, you can't connect to your Server using Office (Network). You'll need to connect via modem and replicate a database from the Server via modem. See the next task to learn how.

2 In your workspace, click the database for which you want to create a local replica. Then, open the **File** menu, choose **Replication**, and from the submenu, choose **New Replica**.

NOTE ▼

If you plan to search the database, you should check the Create full text index for searching box.

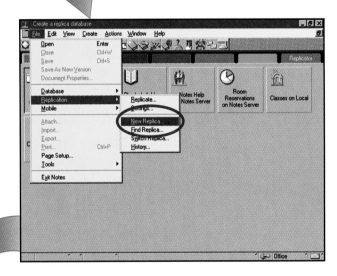

3 In the New Replica dialog box, make sure the Server is set to Local. You don't need to change the Title or the File name unless you want to change them. Choose the **Immediately** option button and then choose **OK**.

4 Notes places a new temporary database icon on the workspace tab, but it doesn't contain a picture (like the letter for a mail database) because Notes has not finished replicating the database, as indicated by the message in the status bar.

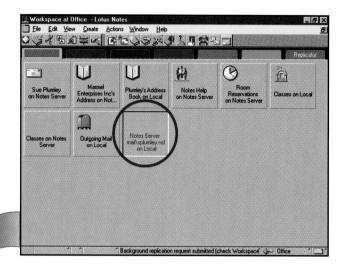

5 Watch the status bar at the bottom of the screen for a message indicating that replication is finished.

WHY WORRY?

If you have previously replicated the selected database, Notes displays a box asking if you want to replace it. Choose Yes to replace it or No to return to the New Replica dialog box.

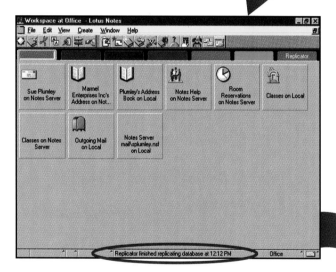

6 Double-click the new icon. Notes opens the database. While Notes opens the database, some other actions occur that you won't see until you close the database. Notes deletes the new icon and changes the title of the original database (the one you replicated) to Local. The original database icon also contains a down arrow on it, which lets you choose a database to open. ■

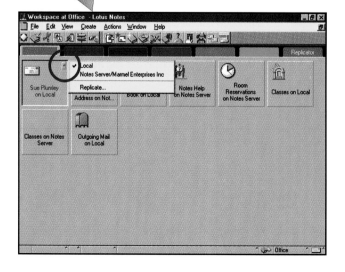

Connecting While on the Road

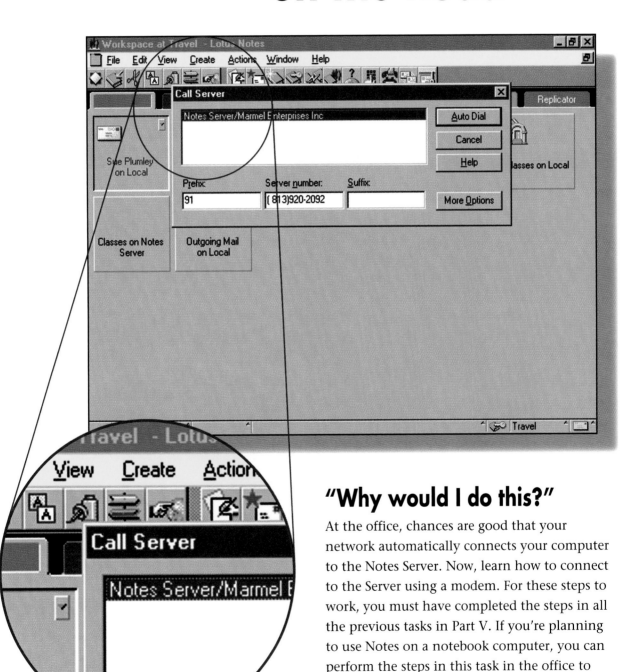

"Why would I do this?"

At the office, chances are good that your network automatically connects your computer to the Notes Server. Now, learn how to connect to the Server using a modem. For these steps to work, you must have completed the steps in all the previous tasks in Part V. If you're planning to use Notes on a notebook computer, you can perform the steps in this task in the office to test and make sure your connection will work.

1 (Optional) If you see `Office` in the box on the lower right portion of the status bar, click the box. Notes displays a pop-up menu. Choose **Travel (Modem)** to change to the Travel location.

You also can open the **File** menu and choose **Mobile**. From the submenu, select **Choose Current Location** and then **Travel (Modem)**.

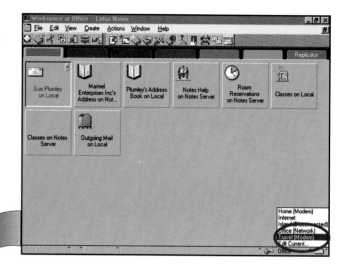

2 Notes displays the Time and Phone Information for Travel dialog box. Complete the information necessary to initiate a phone call from your current location. For example, if you need to dial 9 to get an outside line, enter that in the Dial text box. Then choose **OK**.

NOTE ▼

When you get back to the office, don't forget to change the location back to Office.

3 Open the **File** menu and choose **Mobile**. From the submenu, choose **Call Server**. In the Call Server dialog box, highlight the server you want to call and choose **Auto Dial**. Notes dials your Server. Watch your status bar to see when you are connected.

To hang up from the server, open the **File** menu and choose **Mobile**. From the submenu, choose **Hang Up**. ∎

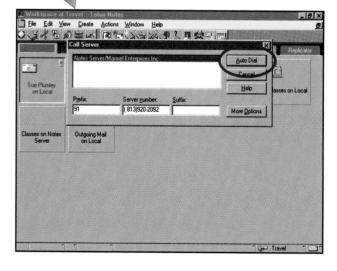

Sending and Receiving Mail on the Road

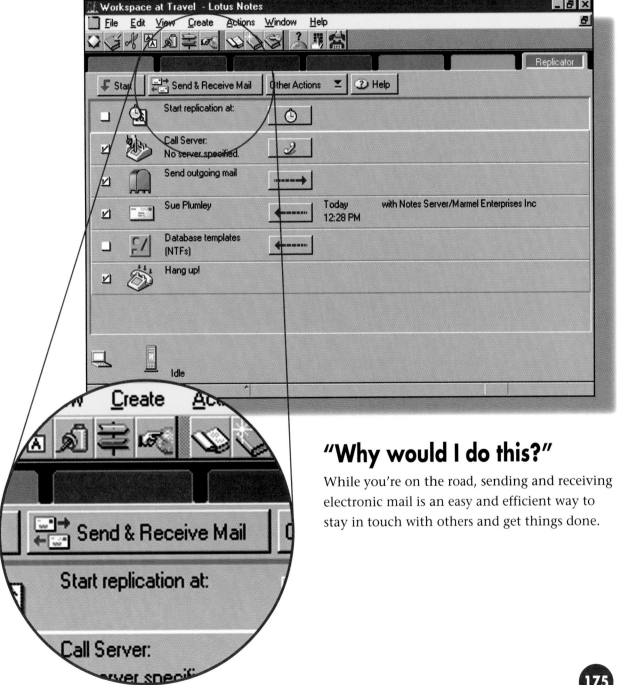

"Why would I do this?"

While you're on the road, sending and receiving electronic mail is an easy and efficient way to stay in touch with others and get things done.

1 Open your local mail database and create any mail you need to send. When you finish a document, choose **Send** or **Send and File**. The mail will appear in the Sent view of your Mail database. Close your mail database when you finish.

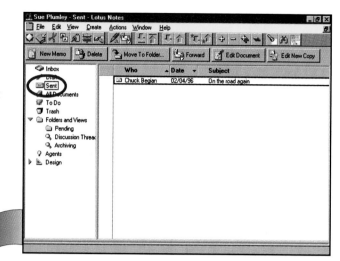

NOTE ▼

See Part II for more information on how to create and send mail.

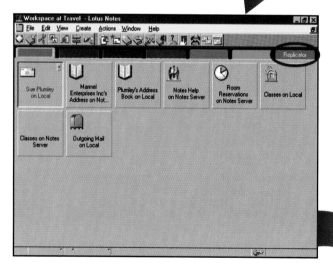

2 Click the **Replicator** tab on your workspace.

WHY WORRY?

To see the mail Notes will send when you connect to the Server, open the Outgoing Mail on Local database—the one containing the picture of the mailbox.

3 Click the **Send & Receive Mail** button. Notes uses the telephone lines to call your Notes Server. Watch the bottom of the screen and the status line for information on the progress of connecting. When Notes finishes sending and receiving mail, it updates the Replicator screen with information on the messages sent and received and then automatically hangs up the call. ■

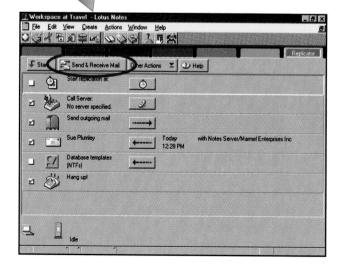

Uploading Changes to Databases

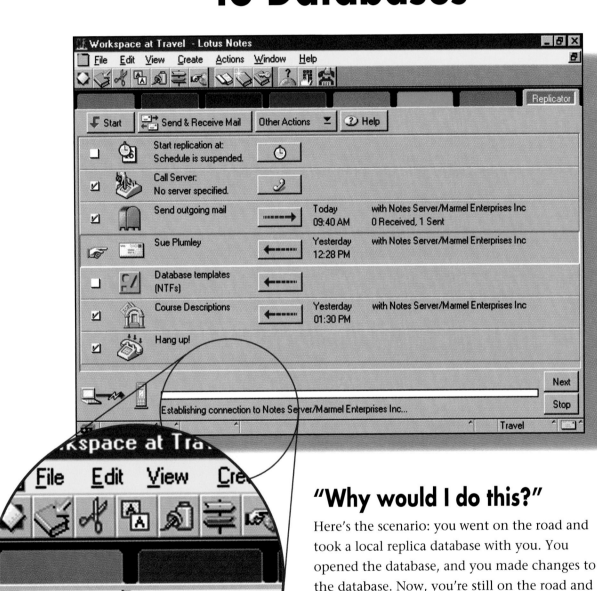

"Why would I do this?"

Here's the scenario: you went on the road and took a local replica database with you. You opened the database, and you made changes to the database. Now, you're still on the road and you need to upload the changes you made to the Notes Server. You need to *replicate* your database onto the server. When you replicate the database, Notes is smart enough to incorporate your changes into the database without changing documents that you didn't modify.

1 Modify a local replica of a database the same way you would modify a database on the server. In this case, we're adding a document to the database. When you finish, use the **Save** and **Close** buttons in the document window to save and close the document.

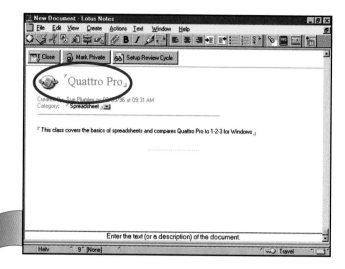

2 Open the **File** menu and choose the **Close** command, or press **Ctrl+W** to close the database and return to the Notes workspace.

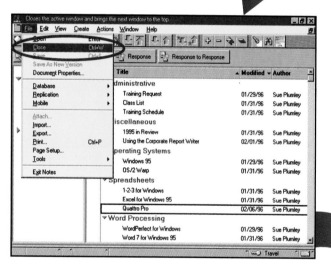

3 Click the **Replicator** tab on your workspace.

> **NOTE** ▼
>
> See Part III for more on how to add documents to a database.

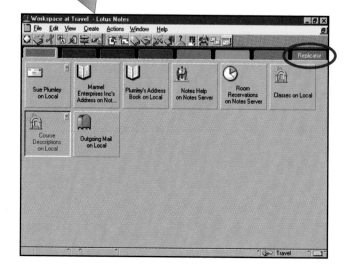

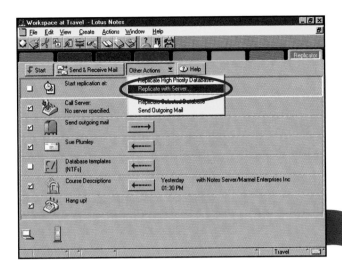

4 Click the **Other Actions** button and choose **Replicate with Server**.

5 From the Server list box, choose the server to which you want to send changes. Choose **OK**.

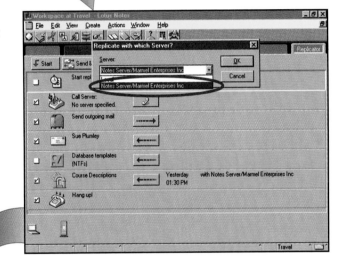

6 Notes uses the telephone lines to call your Notes Server. Watch the bottom of the screen and the status line for information on the progress of connecting.

When Notes finishes replicating the database, it updates the Replicator screen. Then, Notes automatically hangs up the call. If, for some reason, you want to hang up manually, open the **File** menu and choose **Mobile**. From the submenu, choose **Hang Up**. ■

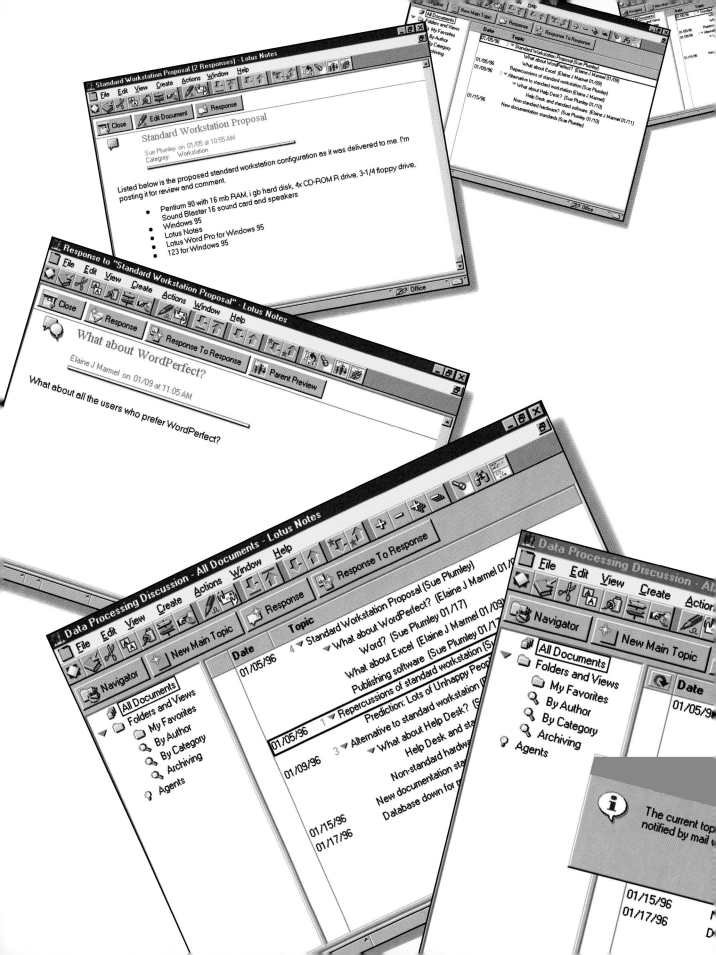

PART VI

Notes and Discussion Groups

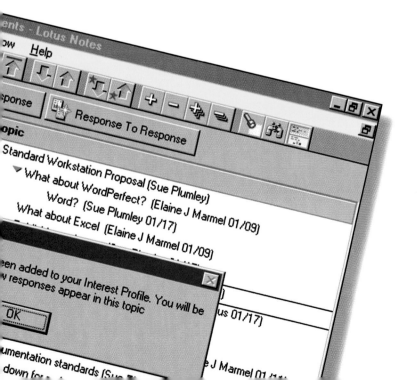

Discussion groups are another type of database in Notes. If you belong to any of the online services or you use the Internet, you may find discussion groups familiar. They are similar to newsgroups on the Internet or forums on CompuServe or America OnLine.

In a discussion group database, typically the documents contain information that the writer needs to share. A marketing group can share information on a marketing campaign they are developing. In many cases, the author of a document hopes to get a response to the document. Suppose, for example, that your company was considering a new health benefits plan. The Health Benefits administrator in Personnel might post a list of the benefits and costs associated with the new plan and then ask for reactions. You would read the document and then respond to it; perhaps you'd even provide reasons explaining why you feel the way you do.

Your response to a document in a discussion group might prompt a third person to comment, either to the Health Benefits administrator or to you. Perhaps the third person would like clarification of an issue you raise.

The point of a discussion group database is to promote communication between Notes users on issues of concern—to provide people with the opportunity to share thoughts and ideas. Think of a discussion group as an informal meeting place, only you don't have to be in the same room with other people to share information and ideas. Topics for discussions are limited only by the people participating, but your company may set down some guidelines to facilitate the process. For example, these guidelines might limit discussion to work issues.

In discussion group databases, you'll find main topic documents, which are used to start a discussion; these documents align at the left edge of the view window. You also see response documents that are used to respond to a main topic document; these documents are indented under the original main topic document to which they respond. Last, you'll see a "response to a response" document, which is indented below the response it answers. You can view documents organized in chronological order by date. You can also view documents by author to see what a particular person has said, or by category, which organizes main topics by subject.

Interest profiles in a discussion group database let you tell Notes about the topics, phrases, keywords, or categories that interest you. Notes uses the interest profile to notify you whenever an item in your interest profile appears in the topics of the database. In your e-mail, you'll find a "newsletter" that contains a document link to the topic in the discussion group database in which you're interested.

Beginners may feel somewhat shy about participating in discussion groups— and that's okay. You can just read information if you want; you don't need to respond. And, you can respond anonymously to a document.

TASK 62

Following the Discussion in a Discussion Group

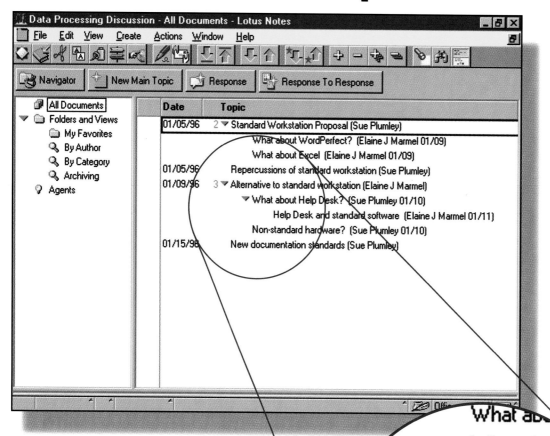

"Why would I do this?"

Joining a discussion group is nothing more than opening the appropriate Notes database. You'll find it easy to follow a discussion if you understand the views available in a discussion group database. In this task, you'll explore the views in a Discussion database and learn to identify main topic documents, response documents, and response to response documents.

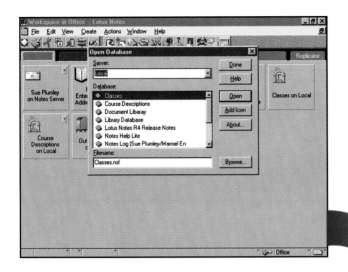

1 Open the **File** menu and choose the **Database** command. From the submenu, choose **Open**. Notes displays the Open Database dialog box.

WHY WORRY?

This example shows a sample discussion database I created based on the Discussion (R4) template that ships with Notes. You can create a database based on this template to practice, or you'll need the name of the discussion database you want to join.

2 In the Server list box, choose the server containing the discussion group you want to join and highlight the database. If Notes prompts you for your password before allowing you to access the server, supply your password. Highlight the discussion database you want to use and click **Open**.

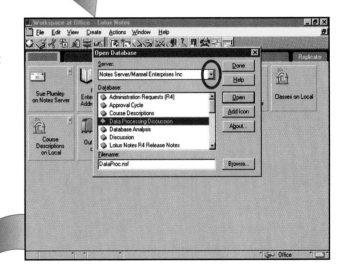

3 Notes adds an icon to your workspace tab and opens the database. You'll see the About this Database document.

4 Press **Ctrl+W**, or open the **File** menu and choose the **Close** command. The views for the database appear. In the default view, the All Documents view, four main topic documents appear in chronological order from earliest to latest.

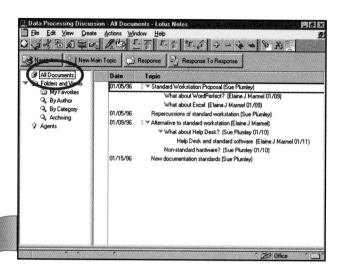

WHY WORRY?

When you open this database, it will probably be empty. Documents appear in the example to make this discussion more clear.

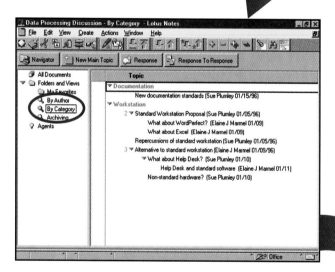

5 In the Navigation pane, click **By Category** to see documents organized by subject. This figure shows two categories: Documentation and Workstation.

NOTE ▼

Responses appear indented below the document to which they respond. In the figure, "What about Excel," is a response to "Standard Workstation Proposal." Response to response documents appear indented below the document they answer. In the figure, "Help Desk and standard software" is a response to response document.

6 In the Navigation pane, click **By Author** to see documents organized by the names of the people who wrote them. ■

NOTE ▼

When you use the Author view, you don't see the hierarchy that indicates whether a document is a main topic, response, or response to response.

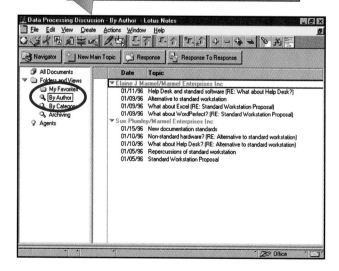

Posting a Message in a Discussion Group

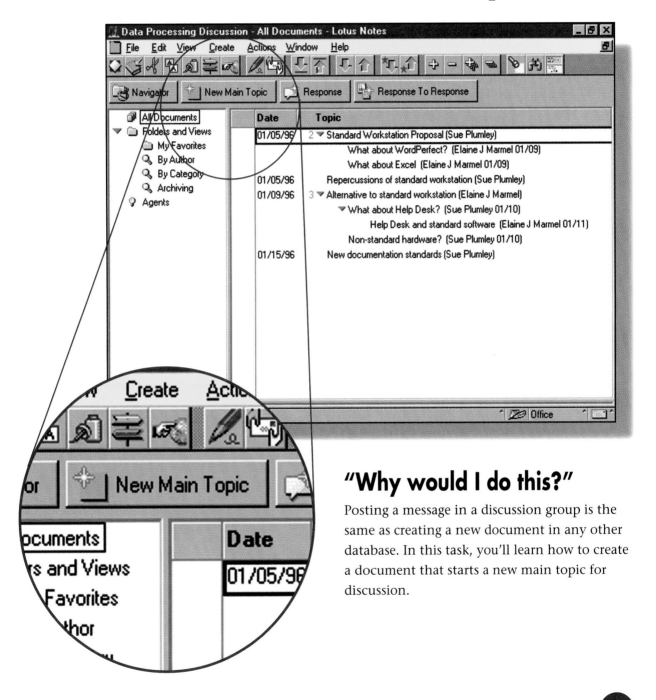

"Why would I do this?"

Posting a message in a discussion group is the same as creating a new document in any other database. In this task, you'll learn how to create a document that starts a new main topic for discussion.

1 Open the Discussion database to any view you choose. Click the **New Main Topic** button in the action bar.

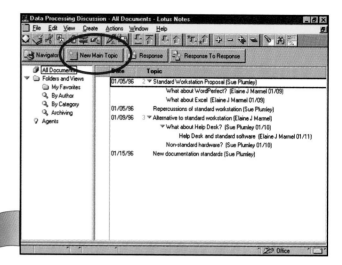

2 In the document window, fill in the information you want to store in the document. The title of the document will be the subject you see in the View pane. If you want to categorize the document, open the category list box and either choose a category or type a new one. Save and close the document using the buttons in the action bar.

3 Your new main topic document appears aligned at the left edge of the topic column. ∎

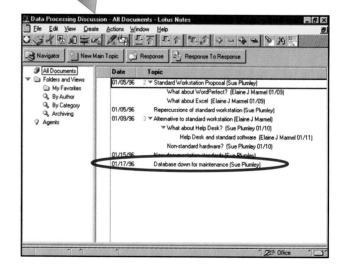

Reading and Responding to a Main Topic Document

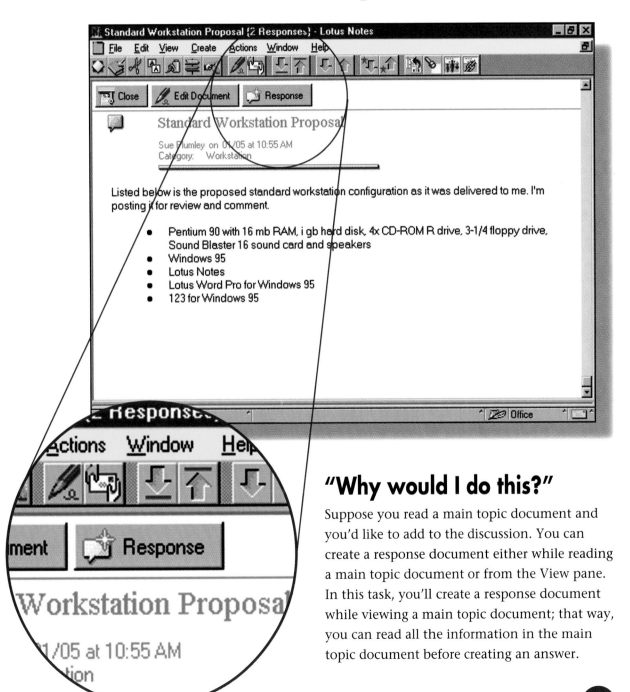

"Why would I do this?"

Suppose you read a main topic document and you'd like to add to the discussion. You can create a response document either while reading a main topic document or from the View pane. In this task, you'll create a response document while viewing a main topic document; that way, you can read all the information in the main topic document before creating an answer.

1 In the View pane, identify the main topic document you want to read.

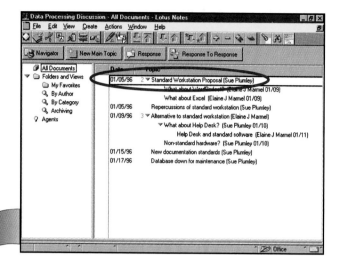

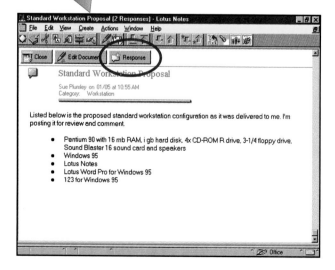

2 Double-click the main topic document you want to read. Notes opens the document so that you can read it.

NOTE ▼

If you already know the content of the main document, you can, instead, click the Response button in the action bar to directly open a response document. If you choose this approach, skip step 3.

3 After reading the document, click the **Response** button in the action bar to open a response document.

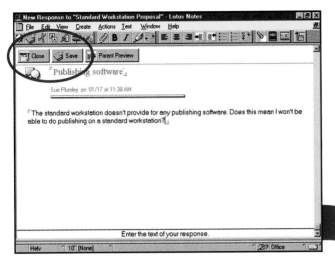

4 Type your response; save and close the document using the buttons on the action bar.

5 After closing the document, Notes redisplays the main topic document. Close it using the action bar.

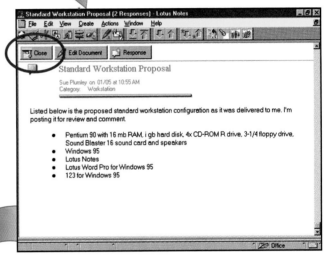

WHY WORRY?

If you chose to open a response document directly in step 2, Notes skips this step.

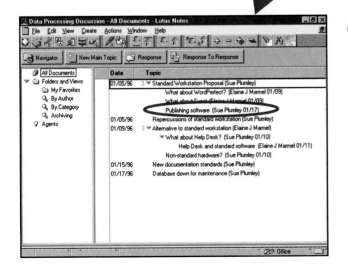

6 In the View pane, your response appears indented below the main topic document to which you responded. ■

TASK 65

Responding to a Response Document

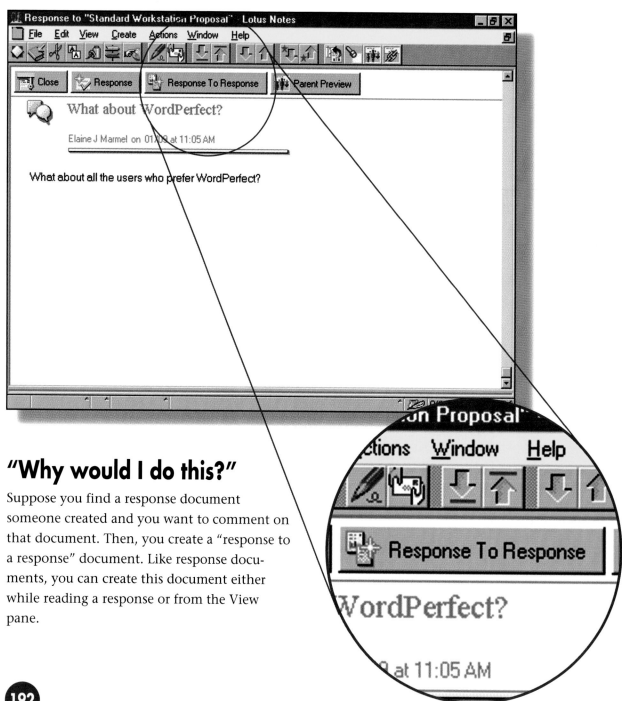

"Why would I do this?"

Suppose you find a response document someone created and you want to comment on that document. Then, you create a "response to a response" document. Like response documents, you can create this document either while reading a response or from the View pane.

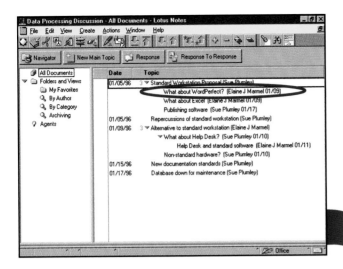

1 In the View pane, identify the response document you want to read.

2 Double-click the response document you want to read. Notes opens the document so that you can read it.

> **NOTE** ▼
>
> If you already know the content of the response document, you can, instead, click the Response To Response button in the action bar to directly open a response to response document. If you choose this approach, skip step 3.

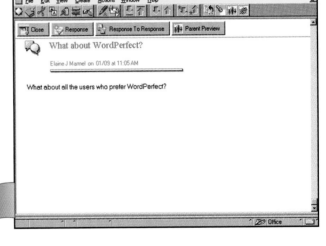

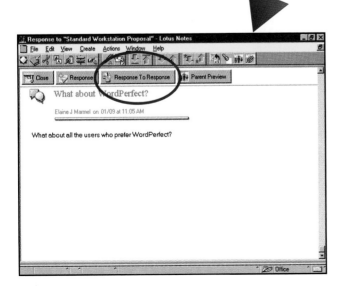

3 After reading the document, click the **Response To Response** button in the action bar to open a response document.

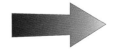

4 Type your response; save and close the document using the buttons on the action bar.

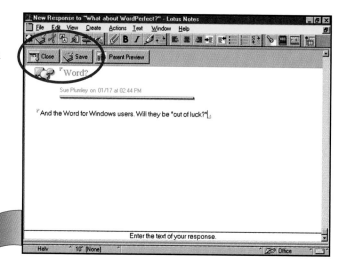

5 After closing the document, Notes redisplays the Response document. Close it using the **Close** button on the action bar.

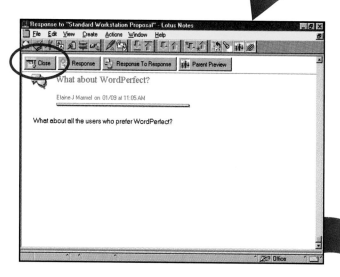

WHY WORRY?

If you chose to open a response to response document directly in step 2, Notes skips this step.

6 In the View pane, your response appears indented below the response document that you answered. ∎

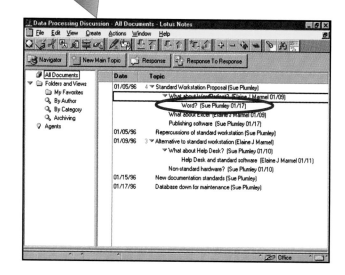

Responding Anonymously

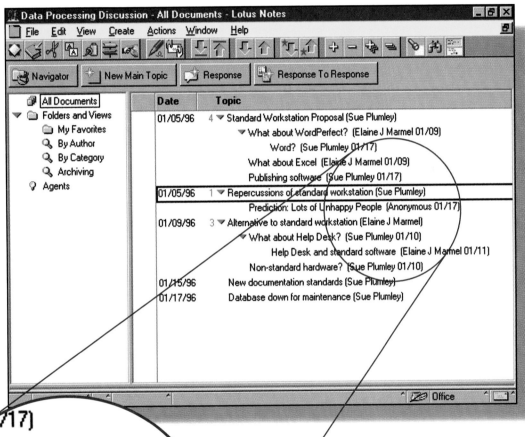

"Why would I do this?"

Suppose you want to respond, but you don't want anybody to know that you're the person responding. Maybe the topic is highly sensitive, or maybe you're just shy. You can create either a response document or a response to a response document that keeps your identity anonymous.

1 Highlight the document to which you want to create an anonymous response (or response to response).

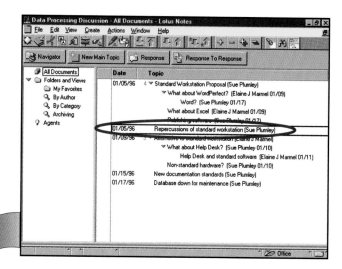

2 Open the **Create** menu and choose **Other**.

3 In the Other dialog box, choose the type of anonymous document you want to create. Choose **OK**.

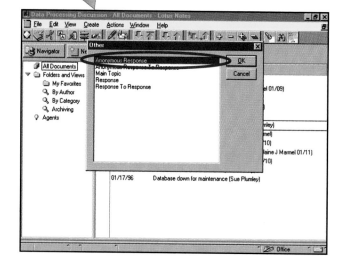

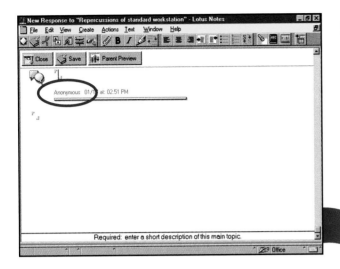

4 Notes displays a document similar to the one you see in this figure, where the author is Anonymous. Complete, save, and close the document.

5 The View pane reappears. Your document, with an author of Anonymous, appears below the document to which you responded. ■

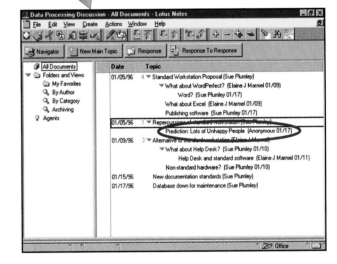

Letting Notes Find Topics That Interest You

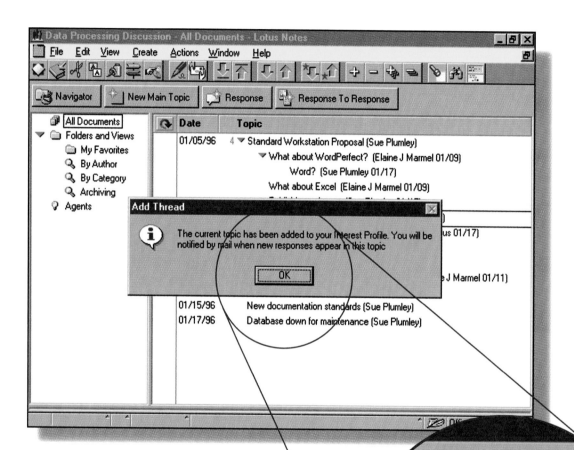

"Why would I do this?"

You can let Notes help you find topics in a discussion database that are of particular interest to you. To let Notes do the work, set up an interest profile, in which you identify information you want Notes to watch for in the database. When Notes comes across a document that meets your criteria, Notes notifies you. And, you can monitor a particular discussion thread (main topic and responses) by adding that thread to your interest profile.

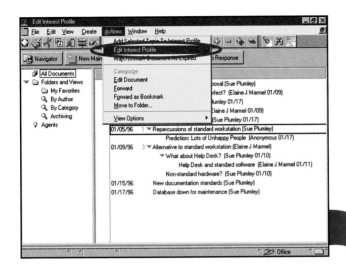

1 Open the discussion database; then open the **Actions** menu and choose **Edit Interest Profile**.

2 In the interest profile, you can ask Notes to inform you about new documents that contain your name, are written by a particular author, appear in particular categories, or contain certain words or phrases. Enter your interests in the brackets, save, and close the interest profile.

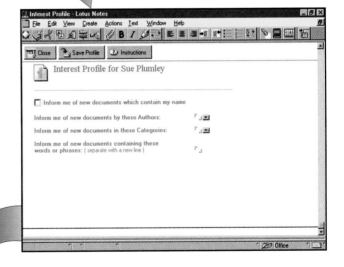

3 To add a discussion thread to your interest profile, highlight that thread.

4 Open the **Actions** menu and choose **Add Selected Topic To Interest Profile**.

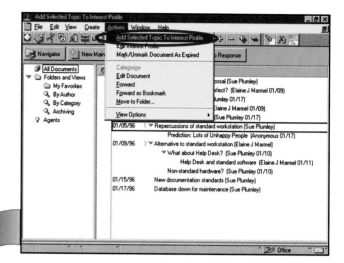

5 Notes informs you after adding the thread that you'll be notified by mail of new responses.

6 If you reopen your interest profile, you'll see the topic of the thread you just added at the bottom of the profile. ∎

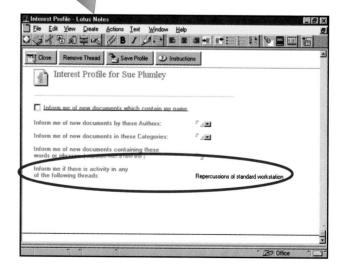

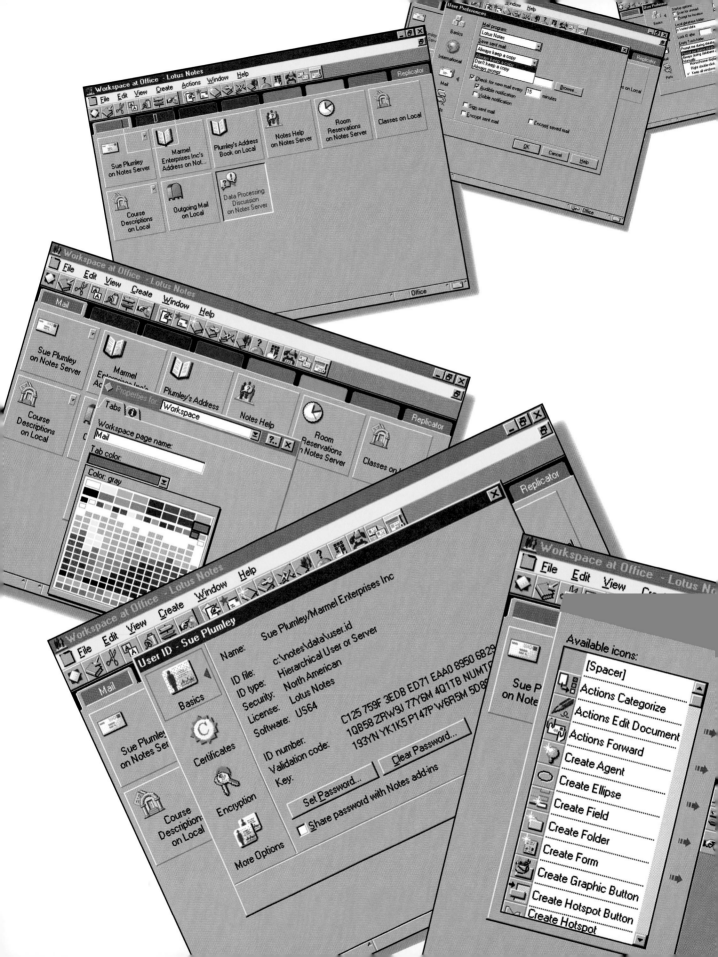

PART VII

Customizing the Notes Workspace

n Part VII, you learn how to customize your Notes workspace. You can, for example, set options that tell Notes when to empty trash and actually delete documents you have marked for deletion. You also have the option to keep copies of the mail you send.

Another easy way to customize your workspace is to place text labels on the folder tabs of your workspace to help with organization. Once you have labeled the workspace tabs, you can move databases back and forth from one tab to another. Keeping similar databases grouped together makes data easier to find.

PASSWORD

As part of the actions you take to customize your workspace, you should change your password. Most system administrators set user passwords to some default value, and encourage users to change their passwords as soon as they can. Notes makes it easy for you to change your personal password whenever you like.

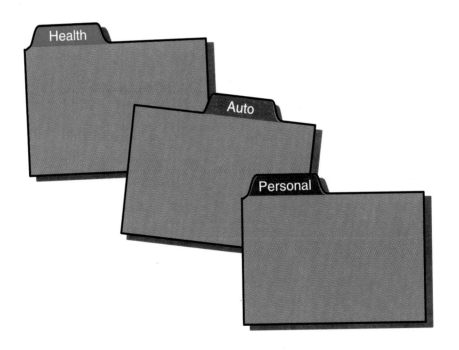

Last, as promised in the beginning of the book, at the end of this part, you will learn how to change the appearance of the database icons and the workspace background. When you first install Lotus Notes, the database icons have a three-dimensional appearance and the workspace looks marbled or textured. To save some strain on the eyes, I changed this default appearance and showed the workspace background as plain gray, with the database icons appearing as simple squares. Try using Notes with the textured setting for a while and then switch to the plain setting to decide which you like best.

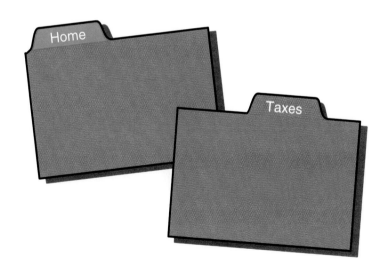

Setting Options for Trash

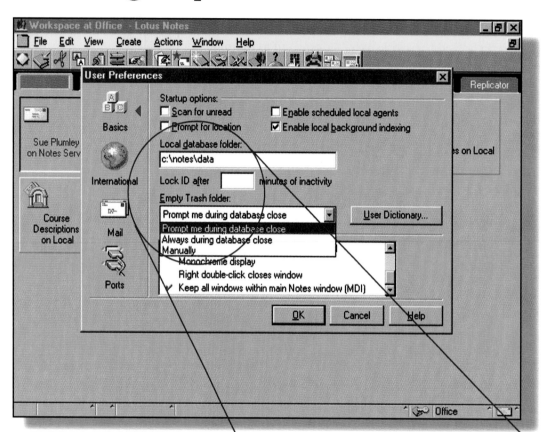

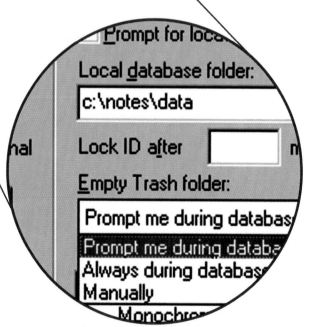

"Why would I do this?"

When you mark a document for deletion, Notes does not immediately delete the document. By default, Notes waits until you exit the database and prompts you to delete marked documents as you exit. You can change this default so that Notes prompts you as you exit a database or so that you must manually empty trash.

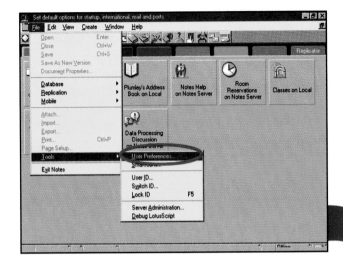

1 Open the **File** menu and choose **Tools**. From the Tools menu, choose **User Preferences**.

2 In the User Preferences dialog box, open the **Empty Trash folder** list box to select an option. Choose **OK** to save your selection.

If you choose Manually, you will need to place documents you want to delete in a Trash folder or mark them for deletion. Then, press **F9** to refresh the screen and actually delete the documents.

If you choose to be prompted to delete as you close a database, Notes displays a reminder message asking if you want to delete marked documents. Choose **Yes** or **No**, as appropriate.

If you choose Always during database close, Notes deletes all documents you marked when you close the database—without prompting you. ■

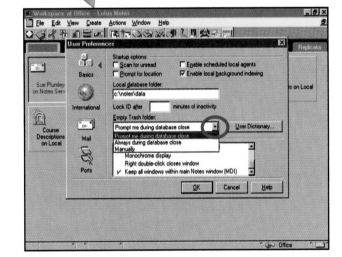

Keeping Copies of Mail You Send

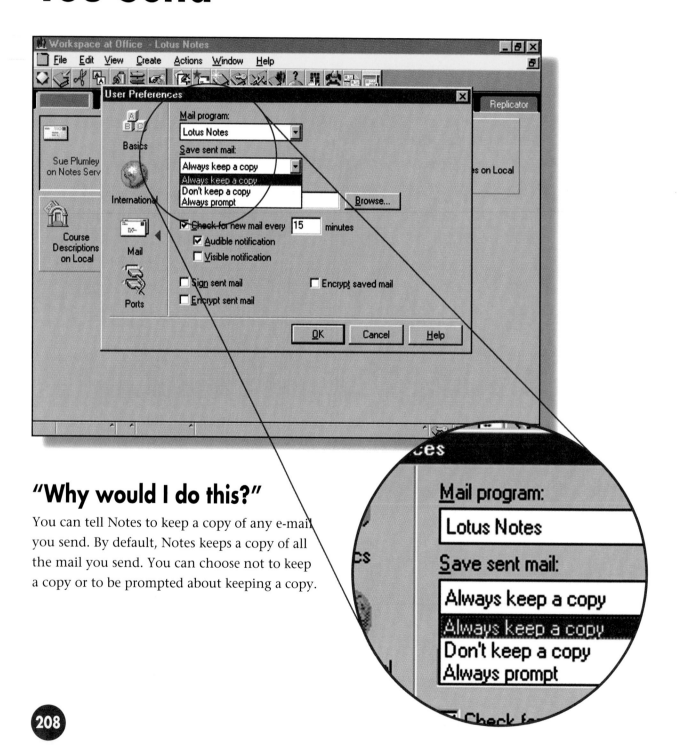

"Why would I do this?"

You can tell Notes to keep a copy of any e-mail you send. By default, Notes keeps a copy of all the mail you send. You can choose not to keep a copy or to be prompted about keeping a copy.

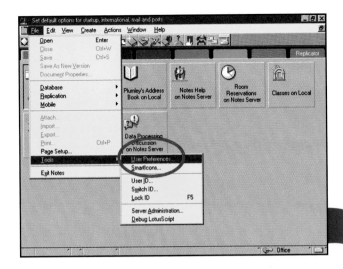

1 Open the **File** menu and choose **Tools**. From the Tools menu, choose **User Preferences**.

2 In the User Preferences dialog box, click the **Mail** icon at the left side of the box to see mail options.

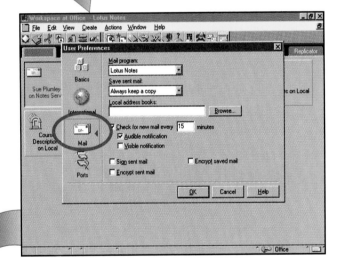

3 Open the Save sent mail list box to see your choices. After you make a selection, choose **OK** to save it. ∎

Moving Databases Between Workspace Pages

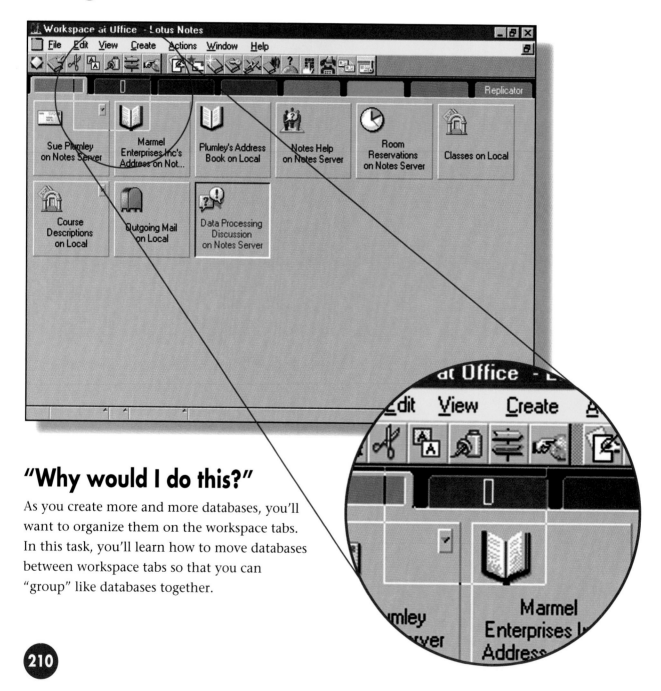

"Why would I do this?"

As you create more and more databases, you'll want to organize them on the workspace tabs. In this task, you'll learn how to move databases between workspace tabs so that you can "group" like databases together.

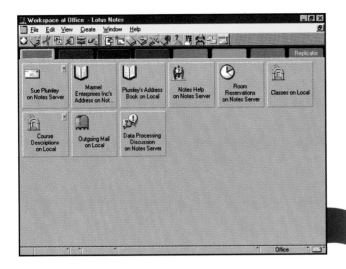

1 Display the workspace tab containing the database you'd like to move.

2 Highlight the database you want to move, drag it up to the workspace tab on which you want to place it, and drop it. As you drag, the mouse pointer will change to a hand and you'll see the outline of the database icon.

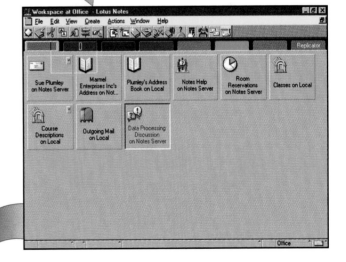

WHY WORRY?

You can identify the tab Notes has selected because you'll see a small white square in the center of the selected tab as you drag the database onto a tab.

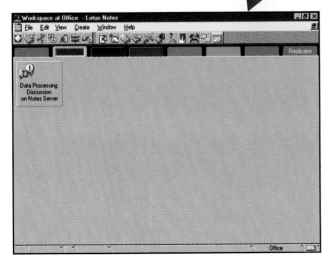

3 Click the tab onto which you moved the database to see the database on that tab. ■

Modifying Workspace Tabs

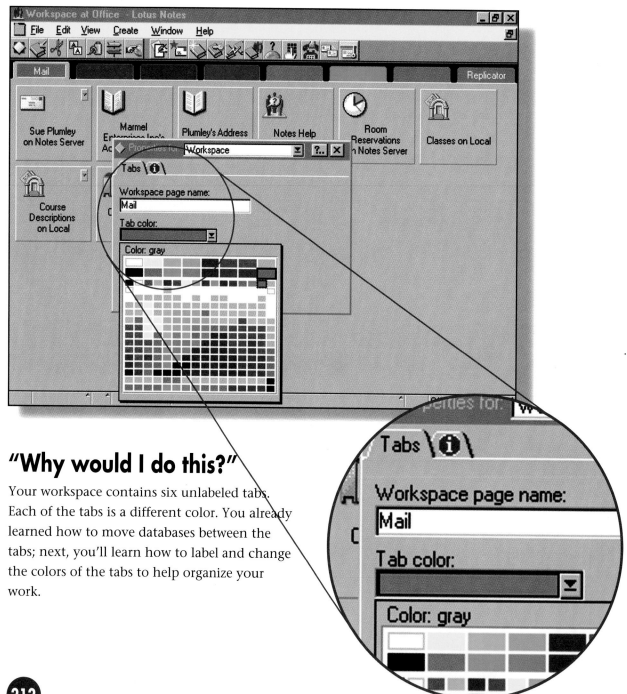

"Why would I do this?"

Your workspace contains six unlabeled tabs. Each of the tabs is a different color. You already learned how to move databases between the tabs; next, you'll learn how to label and change the colors of the tabs to help organize your work.

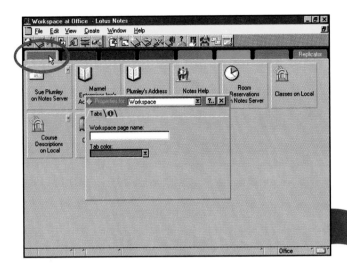

1 Double-click the workspace tab you want to modify. The Workspace Properties InfoBox appears.

2 To label the tab, type a name for the workspace tab in the Workspace page name text box. Notes updates the tab.

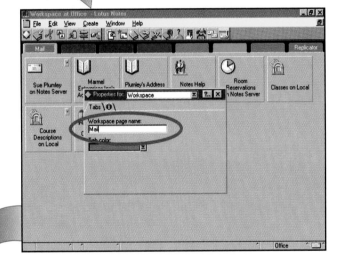

WHY WORRY?

To label and change the color of other tabs, just click on the tab while the Workspace Properties InfoBox is open. Notes will show information for the currently displayed tab.

3 To change the tab color, open the tab color list box and select a color. Notes updates the tab before you close the InfoBox.

Choose the **Close** (**X**) button to close the Properties InfoBox. ■

Changing Your Personal Password

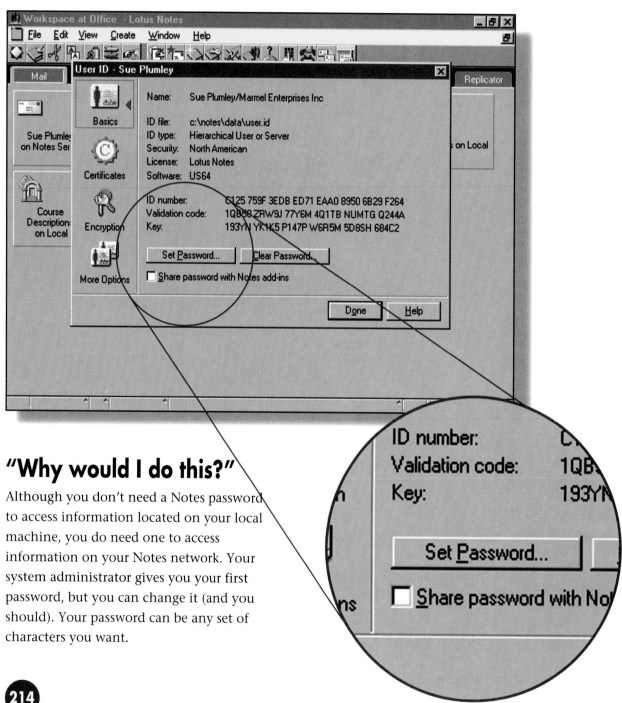

"Why would I do this?"

Although you don't need a Notes password to access information located on your local machine, you do need one to access information on your Notes network. Your system administrator gives you your first password, but you can change it (and you should). Your password can be any set of characters you want.

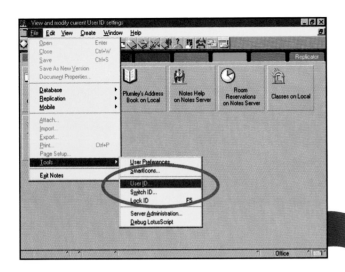

1 Open the **File** menu and choose **Tools**. From the Tools submenu, choose **User ID**.

2 Notes prompts you for your current password. After you supply your password, choose **OK**.

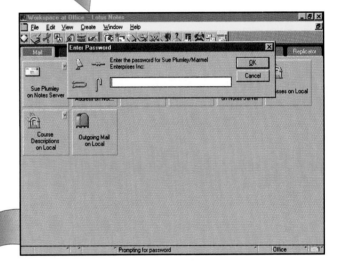

3 Notes displays the User ID dialog box, where you can set your password. Click the **Set Password** command button.

4 Notes displays the Enter Password dialog box. This is the same dialog box Notes prompted you for in step 2. Type your current password and choose **OK**. Notes displays the Set Password dialog box.

WHY WORRY?

Your administrator controls the required length of your password. You may see a different number, such as 8, for the minimum number of required characters.

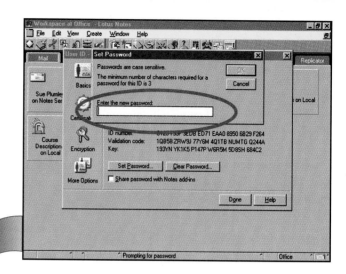

5 Type your new password and choose **OK**. Notes asks you to confirm the password by typing it again.

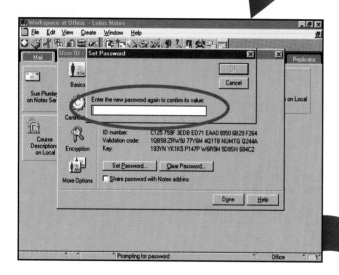

6 After you type the new password and choose **OK**, Notes redisplays the User ID dialog box, from which you can choose **Done**. ■

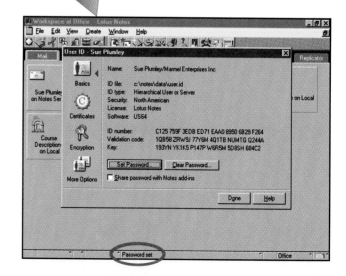

Changing Your Workspace Background

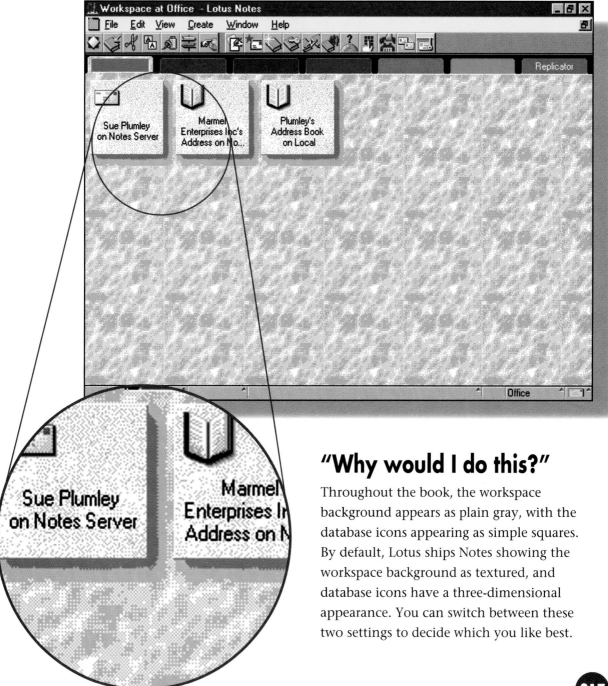

"Why would I do this?"

Throughout the book, the workspace background appears as plain gray, with the database icons appearing as simple squares. By default, Lotus ships Notes showing the workspace background as textured, and database icons have a three-dimensional appearance. You can switch between these two settings to decide which you like best.

1 Open the **File** menu and choose the **Tools** command. From the submenu, choose **User Preferences**.

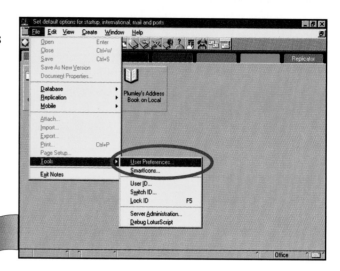

2 In the User Preferences dialog box that appears, search the Advanced options list box until you find Textured Workspace.

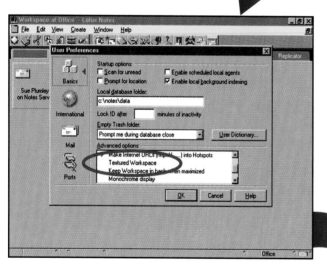

3 If you place a check next to the option and choose **OK**, the Notes workspace will appear textured and database icons will look three-dimensional like the ones in this figure. ■

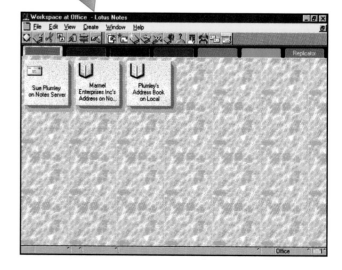

PART VIII

Reference

▼ Installing Notes on a Workstation

▼ Glossary

Installing Notes on a Workstation

Following are the steps you can use to install Lotus Notes to a local area network (LAN) workstation, connected to the server with cables, or as a dial-up workstation, connected to the server by phone lines.

The Notes server must be up and running before you install Notes to the LAN workstation. Additionally, you should temporarily disable any screen savers and virus-detection software; make sure no programs are running on the workstation. As you install the software, you may need additional information such as your password; contact your system administrator.

To install notes on a Windows 95 workstation, follow these steps:

1. From the Windows 95 desktop, choose the **Start** button and the **Run** command.

2. Insert the Lotus CD or disk 1 in the drive and enter the *drive:\directory*install command, for example: d:\win32\install, and press **Enter**. If you're using floppy disks to install, insert new disks in the floppy drive as prompted.

3. When prompted, enter your name and company name, and choose **Next**.

4. Choose **Yes** to confirm the names or **No** to re-enter them.

5. When prompted, choose the **Standard Install** option and choose **Next**.

6. Continue installation, answering the on-screen prompts as necessary.

Glossary

ACL (Access Control List) The list of users allowed to use a database. The ACL lists who is allowed to access the database and what kind of access they have. Access can range from No Access to Manager.

action bar The bar of buttons above the View pane that contain various actions you can take, such as Create a New Document.

Address Book A database that contains the names and e-mail addresses of Notes users. It can also include physical addresses and phone numbers. The Address Book on the Server contains the names and e-mail addresses of all Notes users on the network. Notes uses the Address Book to route mail.

attachment A file included in a Notes document. To send a file to another Notes user, you can send the file as an attachment in an e-mail message.

BCC (Blind Carbon Copy) Sends a copy of an e-mail message to a recipient(s) whose name(s) and address(es) appear in the BCC field without any of the other recipients being aware of it.

CC (Carbon Copy) Sends a copy of an e-mail message to the recipient(s) whose name(s) and address(es) appear in the CC field.

client A computer or workstation that connects to a server. Usually, your computer is a client that connects to a server located somewhere else.

database A Notes file, represented by a database icon. Notes databases are like compartments and store documents. Typically, databases are located on servers and accessed by clients from all over the network. You can read a description of a particular database using the About button in the Open Database dialog box.

database design Determines how the users read, input, and modify information in a database. A database design consists of design elements such as fields, forms, views, and macros.

database icon Square icon that represents a Notes database. Database icons contain pictures and descriptive titles. Optionally, the number of unread messages can be displayed on the icon.

DocLink A small icon that appears in a database document. When you double-click the DocLink icon, Notes switches to the document referenced by the DocLink.

document A completed form in a Notes database.

field   A place in a document containing information. Some fields allow you to type into them, and others have formulas that perform calculations.

form   The foundation of a document. The form determines how fields are displayed and how information can be entered into them.

full text index   A listing of all words in the database you can use to search documents in a database.

full text search   A query against the full text index to locate documents matching specified words, phrases, numbers, or dates.

groupware   An application that helps people work collaboratively with electronic information. Lotus Notes is an example of groupware.

LAN   (Local Area Network) Servers and clients connected by cables or telephone wires for the purpose of sharing data. The servers typically stay logged on to the LAN, so that the information in their databases can be accessed at any time. Clients typically log on and off of the LAN as necessary.

modem   A device that attaches to a computer to allow for remote communication via phone lines.

Navigation pane   The area on the left side of the screen when you open a database. The Navigation pane may contain icons or folders. Use the Navigation pane to switch folders and display database contents in different ways.

password   An encrypted text string that permits use of a user ID to authorized persons and, conversely, denies use of a user ID to unauthorized persons. Typically, Notes users each have a single User ID, which they do not share.

pop-up   Area on a document that you can click for additional information. The document's author can place pop-ups almost anywhere on the document. Usually, you see pop-ups as a green rectangle surrounding text.

Preview pane   A pane that can appear at the bottom of the screen. The preview pane displays the contents of the document currently highlighted in the View pane.

record   A record is the same thing as a document. See *document*.

remote workstation   A computer that connects to the network via modem.

server   A computer that stores data for use by clients. In Notes, the server also authenticates your User ID when you attempt to access the server; you must have a valid User ID in order to access any server. Notes databases are typically located on servers.

SmartIcons   A row of small square icons (default location is at the top of the screen) that you can click to perform Notes menu commands.

template   A database without records that you can use as a model when creating a new database. Templates contain a complete set of design elements. Notes ships with many templates. You see a list of available templates on your own machine in the New Database dialog box. If you switch to the server, you'll see a list of templates available on the server in the New Database dialog box.

User ID   An encrypted, unique password that allows the person who knows the password access to Notes servers and databases.

view   A display of documents in a database. Views contain documents that are sorted, totaled, or grouped together in almost any logical manner.

View pane   The right side of the screen when you open a database. The View pane typically lists documents, and the order of the documents depends on which folder you select in the Navigation pane.

workspace   The window displayed when Notes is first activated. The workspace has seven tabbed pages, including the Replicator tab. You can view the different contents of a workspace tab by clicking the tab.

Index

W-X-Y-Z

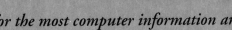

PLUG YOURSELF INTO...

THE MACMILLAN INFORMATION SUPERLIBRARY™

Free information and vast computer resources from the world's leading computer book publisher—online!

FIND THE BOOKS THAT ARE RIGHT FOR YOU!

A complete online catalog, plus sample chapters and tables of contents give you an in-depth look at *all* of our books, including hard-to-find titles. It's the best way to find the books you need!

- **STAY INFORMED** with the latest computer industry news through our online newsletter, press releases, and customized Information SuperLibrary Reports.

- **GET FAST ANSWERS** to your questions about MCP books and software.

- **VISIT** our online bookstore for the latest information and editions!

- **COMMUNICATE** with our expert authors through e-mail and conferences.

- **DOWNLOAD SOFTWARE** from the immense MCP library:
  - Source code and files from MCP books
  - The best shareware, freeware, and demos

- **DISCOVER HOT SPOTS** on other parts of the Internet.

- **WIN BOOKS** in ongoing contests and giveaways!

TO PLUG INTO MCP: →

GOPHER: gopher.mcp.com
FTP: ftp.mcp.com

WORLD WIDE WEB: **http://www.mcp.com**

Complete and Return this Card
for a *FREE* Computer Book Catalog

Thank you for purchasing this book! You have purchased a superior computer book written expressly for your needs. To continue to provide the kind of up-to-date, pertinent coverage you've come to expect from us, we need to hear from you. Please take a minute to complete and return this self-addressed, postage-paid form. In return, we'll send you a free catalog of all our computer books on topics ranging from word processing to programming and the internet.

Mr. ☐   Mrs. ☐   Ms. ☐   Dr. ☐

Name (first) ☐☐☐☐☐☐☐☐☐☐☐☐   (M.I.) ☐   (last) ☐☐☐☐☐☐☐☐☐☐☐☐☐☐☐☐☐☐☐☐☐☐☐☐☐

Address ☐☐☐☐☐☐☐☐☐☐☐☐☐☐☐☐☐☐☐☐☐☐☐☐☐☐☐☐☐☐☐☐☐☐☐☐☐

☐☐☐☐☐☐☐☐☐☐☐☐☐☐☐☐☐☐☐☐☐☐☐☐☐☐☐☐☐☐☐☐☐☐☐☐☐

City ☐☐☐☐☐☐☐☐☐☐☐☐☐☐☐☐☐☐   State ☐☐   Zip ☐☐☐☐☐ ☐☐☐☐

Phone ☐☐☐ ☐☐☐ ☐☐☐☐   Fax ☐☐☐ ☐☐☐ ☐☐☐☐

Company Name ☐☐☐☐☐☐☐☐☐☐☐☐☐☐☐☐☐☐☐☐☐☐☐☐☐☐☐☐☐☐☐☐☐

E-mail address ☐☐☐☐☐☐☐☐☐☐☐☐☐☐☐☐☐☐☐☐☐☐☐☐☐☐☐☐☐☐☐☐☐

1. Please check at least (3) influencing factors for purchasing this book.

Front or back cover information on book .... ☐
Special approach to the content .... ☐
Completeness of content .... ☐
Author's reputation .... ☐
Publisher's reputation .... ☐
Book cover design or layout .... ☐
Index or table of contents of book .... ☐
Price of book .... ☐
Special effects, graphics, illustrations .... ☐
Other (Please specify): _____ ☐

2. How did you first learn about this book?

Saw in Macmillan Computer Publishing catalog .... ☐
Recommended by store personnel .... ☐
Saw the book on bookshelf at store .... ☐
Recommended by a friend .... ☐
Received advertisement in the mail .... ☐
Saw an advertisement in: _____ ☐
Read book review in: _____ ☐
Other (Please specify): _____ ☐

3. How many computer books have you purchased in the last six months?

This book only .... ☐   3 to 5 books .... ☐
2 books .... ☐   More than 5 .... ☐

4. Where did you purchase this book?

Bookstore .... ☐
Computer Store .... ☐
Consumer Electronics Store .... ☐
Department Store .... ☐
Office Club .... ☐
Warehouse Club .... ☐
Mail Order .... ☐
Direct from Publisher .... ☐
Internet site .... ☐
Other (Please specify): _____ ☐

5. How long have you been using a computer?

☐ Less than 6 months   ☐ 6 months to a year
☐ 1 to 3 years   ☐ More than 3 years

6. What is your level of experience with personal computers and with the subject of this book?

	With PCs	With subject of book
New	☐	☐
Casual	☐	☐
Accomplished	☐	☐
Expert	☐	☐

Source Code ISBN: 0-7897-0756-X

7. Which of the following best describes your job title?

- Administrative Assistant ☐
- Coordinator ☐
- Manager/Supervisor ☐
- Director ☐
- Vice President ☐
- President/CEO/COO ☐
- Lawyer/Doctor/Medical Professional ☐
- Teacher/Educator/Trainer ☐
- Engineer/Technician ☐
- Consultant ☐
- Not employed/Student/Retired ☐
- Other (Please specify): _____ ☐

8. Which of the following best describes the area of the company your job title falls under?

- Accounting ☐
- Engineering ☐
- Manufacturing ☐
- Operations ☐
- Marketing ☐
- Sales ☐
- Other (Please specify): _____ ☐

9. What is your age?

- Under 20 ☐
- 21-29 ☐
- 30-39 ☐
- 40-49 ☐
- 50-59 ☐
- 60-over ☐

10. Are you:

- Male ☐
- Female ☐

11. Which computer publications do you read regularly? (Please list)

_____
_____
_____
_____
_____
_____
_____
_____
_____

Comments: _____
_____
_____

Fold here and scotch-tape to mail.